THE ABSOLUTE CERTAINTY OF LIFE AFTER DEATH

JUST A NOVEL

Don Wilton

Published in Nashville, Tennessee, by Thomas Nelson. Thomas Nelson is a trademark of Thomas Nelson, Inc.

Thomas Nelson, Inc. titles may be purchased in bulk for educational, business, fund-raising, or sales promotional use. For information, please email nelsonministryservices@thomasnelson.com.

ISBN-10: 0849919940
ISBN-13: 9780849919947

This book is dedicated to all the people we have known and loved who have taught us how to die! We will see you again!

Acknowledgements

I really want to thank a number of people who have meant so much to me as I wrote this novel about life after death. First, my Lord and Savior, who has given me the privilege of speaking His truth about life after death with a deep and abiding conviction that God's matchless love is evidence that He desires that no person should ever go to a Christ-less eternity. Second, the countless thousands who have heard me preach on the subject literally around the world. The feedback has been overwhelming and the response to every invitation to accept the Lord Jesus Christ as Savior has been joyfully significant. Third, Sharon Brisken, my personal secretary, who is always at her post and is tireless in her devotion to assist me in every way. Fourth, Randy Elliott, Vice President at Thomas Nelson, who has become more than just a publisher to me—rather he is my brother and friend. I am deeply grateful for the significant role he has played in the publishing of this novel. Finally, my wife, Karyn. I can never adequately express what she means to me. She has listened to more stories than I can ever imagine and her counsel, encouragement and unapologetic love have sustained me and compelled me to keep serving our Savior.

Introduction

———

Most people are fascinated by the subject of life after death. I know this to be true because I have had the privilege of teaching and preaching on this subject for many years. Whether in a seminary classroom setting or in a massive crusade in a stadium, or in a local church revival, or in my own pulpit—life after death is intriguing! Most people want to know! For years I have studied the subject and tried to get a handle on it. The problem is none of us have ever actually died and then lived to tell about it! But some of us have certainly had near-death experiences!

I am just one of many!

In the summer of 2003, I boarded a bus bound for Texas with over 100 senior high students from our church to go and minister to inmates incarcerated for crimes against their fellow man. From the start, I knew something was wrong with me. As Mirror Image sang and performed and as I stood and spoke the truth of God's love, I could feel my left arm tightening up. Most of my enjoyable delights took a back seat to the point that even my usual roller-coaster rides at Six Flags were passed by. By the time we made it back to Spartanburg, my arm had swollen to the size of my legs. The vascular surgeon took one look at it and ordered me into surgery immediately. I had two massive blood clots in my upper shoulder, probably caused by a motorcycle accident when I was just a teenager. I heard him tell my wife just how serious this was and how easily I could have died.

The four hour surgery left me feeling like I was hovering between life and death. And what if I did die? I could see the doctor with his arm on Karyn's shoulder telling her, "I'm so sorry. He didn't make it!" I could see myself lying there on that table—but I was not there. All I did know was I had a peace and calm in my heart I had never experienced! There was no sadness or sorrow, not even for my wife. There was simply an unsurpassed joy and calm.

Suddenly I became aware of where I was again. Everything came back into focus. Intensive care was next. My total recovery followed and the Lord spared me to continue to live in this life according to His purpose.

As I sat in my bed, I picked up a pen and started writing about The Absolute Certainty of Life after Death. The story just flowed out of my heart. I never stopped until it was complete.

This book is just a novel.

Taken from the story Jesus told us about the rich man and Lazarus, I wrote a fictional account of two men who lived on this earth and then died. One went to heaven and the other went to hell. That's what Jesus said!

People want to know! I want to know! How come we always say things like, "I promise you—you will see your loved ones in heaven!" A question I hear all the time is, "What happens the moment you die?" "What happens to a person when they go through death?" "Where, exactly, do we go?" "Do dead people know what's going on down here on earth?" "How do we know these things?" "Aren't all people going to end up in the same place—eventually?" "Why all the fuss?" Or, how about this one: "How can you say God is a God of love and mercy and yet also say God sends people to hell?"

These are great questions. And there are hundreds more. That's why I am currently writing a follow up to this novel: The Absolute Certainty of Life after Death: Just the Facts! This is a book based solely on the absolute truths of God's Word.

In this novel, I have taken the lives of two men from birth to death to heaven and to hell. I have tried to depict the reality of life through their eyes because they are everyman! You are reading about you and me! The places they find themselves are places very familiar to me, but I make no claim whatsoever as to the exactness of every lamp post and turn in the street. This is a fictional story based on a true story Jesus shared with us. Jesus certainly had no need to concoct some fabricated account of two imaginary men in an effort to provide us with some means to "jolt" sinful man into accepting Jesus into their hearts and lives so as to avoid the pits of hell! Not on your life! Jesus is God and in Him there is no lie!

So take this novel, find a good chair and read it. And if you do not know the Lord Jesus Christ as your Savior, take action immediately. I call it by the letters ACT.

A   Acknowledge your sin (Romans 3:23: "For all have sinned and fall short of the glory of God.")

C   Confess your sin only to Jesus (John 14:6: "I am the way, the truth and the life. No man comes to the Father but by Me.")

T   Trust God to do what He says He will do. (Ephesians 2:8-9: "For it is by grace you have been saved, through faith—and this is not from yourselves, it is the gift of God—not by works, so that no one can boast.")

If you are willing to ACT, God will save you and you will go to heaven forever. Do this now!

And if you read this book as a believer, please pass it on to someone you love and care for. Their life may depend on it!

PART I

THIS IS A STORY ABOUT TWO MEN.
ONE WAS VERY RICH. THE OTHER WAS
VERY POOR. THEY BOTH DIED.

One

———

Let's face it. Life was good. Extremely good. Some people just have it made, I guess. There he sat. A self made man in many ways although one could not ignore the few lucky breaks that had come his way. When asked, which few people dared to do, he pushed the question away with the slight gesture of a hand more suitable for a king mounted on his throne than someone whose entire fortune had seemed to fall into his lap by some strange coincidence.

That's exactly why he had been such a Walter Cronkite fan all those years.

"That's the way it is" seemed to strike the chord. "On the money," he would tell scores of admirers. Especially his two sons. Not that it did them much good. Especially Rothy...

Amby had caught the idea, that much was obvious. How proud he made his Daddy.

The girls were a different story. His wife just went along with it.

As the private jet with the "Texas Mete" logo brilliantly displayed on both sides took off from the New Orleans Lakefront Airport, its owner sank back in his plush seat with an inner sigh of satisfaction.

Albright A. Rhodes was a multi-millionaire. Some believed he was a billionaire, but without full disclosure no one really knew. Born seventy-nine years ago, to the month, he had every right to look back on his life with a smile of satisfaction. He knew what it was all about. He had walked the road and held his head up high. Very high. A lot of people really appreciated him.

As he gazed out of the window of his jet plane he felt it again. He couldn't quite put his finger on it. He wanted to tell his wife. But, there again, most of his close friends and admirers were surgeons and specialists and such. He'd just give Dr. Michael Harrington a call and then fly him down to the ranch.

He preferred the privacy, anyway.

Two

Even though his father and mother had exchanged harsh words about the naming of their first born son, his father had won the day. Mildred was actually too weak and washed out to argue anyway.

"The boy needs to have a man's name, woman," he scowled.

"Besides he's my first born. And a son at that! Proper thing to do is to name him for his daddy. The folks around here expect it. It's just decent, Mildred!"

The birth had been long and hard. The hardships of living so far out in the country had meant little to her husband. He really liked the old farmstead even though blood sweat and tears had thoroughly washed his own parents' faces many times. The farmstead was in the rolling hills of Texas. All the folks who lived just south of Austin and somewhere north of San Antonio understood the hill thing. Hard to believe considering Texas. But that's the way those folks kind of identified their origin.

Albright arrived accompanied by the screams of his mother and the dogmatic insistence of his father.

He hated the name later on.

His distinguished position in life today was by no means a reflection of the nightmare he endured yesterday. The kids at the country school were merciless. Albright was of medium stature, and, unfortunately, had to wear spectacles from the age of seven. His mother came to this conclusion just by watching the way in which her boy would pull up his nose, squint his eyes and tilt his head when trying to read. His father smacked him more than once because he said his face looked like one of the baby hogs squealing in anger and frustration because one of the other baby hogs had beaten him to the mother's milk bar. He couldn't help it, he pleaded to no avail. Thank goodness for Mammas. Of course, back then in the sticks of Texas, eye doctors were hard to come by. In any case, no one could spell "optometrist" and most of the folks would rather have just "had their eyes seen to" than go and visit some fancy doctor with fancy coat and a fancy name to go along with it. Driving a Ford truck was enough of a lofty ideal anyway.

The problem was the Depression. Even though Albright was a bit on the young side it did not take much to stir his memory. Maybe the name Albright was actually the cause of the Depression, he thought.

He hated it but not as much as his second name. Ambrose! Now at seventy-nine, with a son by the same name, he could smile and almost force a little private haw-haw when he was convinced no-one else was watching. After all, Amby was the apple of his eye. So Mildred and Albright, senior, must have known all along that names carry their weight in gold. It still did not take the hurt and pain away from his growing up years.

And Mildred had this awful drawn out way of calling his name. Especially when he was in trouble or like the time his sister had reported him for spying on her while she was getting changed. He couldn't help it. Those parts of hers were just fascinating. Watching her gave him status, anyway, especially at school. He knew the other boys, particularly the big one with the red hair who always had something to say about Albright's glasses or nose and liked to push him into the garbage cans, would appreciate the details about his sister's parts. In fact he knew he had thrown a bull's eye when the red head and the little squeak who went by the name of Lizard paid him a dime to set up a private viewing of his sister toweling off after her bath. Lizard had established himself as the red head's aide-de-camp or deputy minister of misinformation. Whatever he was did not remove the fact that he was a worm.

No wonder Albright A. Rhodes, now in his seventy-ninth year, still had a real problem with those he referred to as "leaches". His money was his. It was to be dispensed after much research. It always had strings attached. Most people, he thought, had no idea just how difficult it was to be well set, as it were. At least he could see it from both sides. Growing up on the other side gave him somewhat of a perspective on these things.

One thing was for sure. He never "leached." Not once. Not even when Mister Roger took a fancy to him. He was one rich old man with a kind heart. Always treated Albright with respect. When he asked the boy to take care of the dogs when he went away, Albright always did much more than required. He even had to go and talk to the cat every day at five just in case Timberline fell into some kind of cat depression or something. It was always hard work knowing exactly what to say so as to prevent the cat from having to see a shrink or whatever depressed cats do.

Three

When the Red Head and Lizard paid so handsomely for a private viewing, Albright knew exactly how to manage the transaction. Unfortunately the whole affair was marred by the fact that Lizard got so carried away in anticipation of what the boys considered "the first wonder of the world," he forgot to tie his shoelace. Even the very thought of some of those "hidden secrets" had sent his hormones into a frenzy.

The three of them, with Albright in the obviously subservient role, had maneuvered into an excellent position from which to view the marvels of God's creation. The plan was simple.

It just so happened the week's Sunday School lesson was on "God's Loving Kindness." The three troubadours had little difficulty in realizing that God, according to His loving kindness, had positioned Missy's room on the side of the house.

"Told you so, Lizard. That's what Mr. Cameron said in Sunday School and stuff."

"What stuff?"

"God's stuff. The stuff He does so's to make things good and stuff. Like lettin' her room be private next to the corn and stuff."

"Yeh." Lizard agreed quickly. "An' my Mamma told me the stuff girls have like their parts and stuff is all good 'cause God gave it like that to use for good stuff when the right time comes. So I figure Mister Cameron just gave us a heads up so

God would put things and stuff in the right place so's we can see it and stuff."

"Shuddup man! You'll blow our cover!" Albright interjected with the obvious weight of authority.

Not only did her room have a big window but it ran adjacent to the corn field making it totally unnecessary to draw the curtains at any point in time. The dogs would take immediate care of intruders anyway. Albright was their best pal.

And so a make-shift platform of wooden planks, borrowed from the barn, was constructed between two large used gas drums. At precisely eight in the evening, when Albright assured them she would be stripping to take a bath before bedtime, the fearsome three emerged from the corn field on hands and knees like three dogs on the prowl.

They could clearly see the unwitting victim in the window already down to basics. The Red Head whimpered, Lizard almost blew their cover by blurting out something about loving kindness and Albright flung his arms around his dogs to assure them a terrorist attack on the compound was not imminent.

As they began to mount the viewing deck Lizard tripped on his untied shoelace. The three began to fall one at a time like a deck of cards falling from a table. The royal trinity landed with such force on top of all Mr. Rhodes' neatly stacked cans that the entire platform collapsed.

It seemed like the world had suddenly come to an end.

All the reverend had yelled about from the hallowed perch of his pulpit began, all of a sudden, to make sense. This was the moment he had been trying to warn them about. The cans were clashing, all five dogs began to bark in the worst possible way, at least seventeen of the farm cats began imagining the five dogs had finally figured out a way to corner them in a snackbar kind of way, the chickens in the chicken coup were jolted out of their early evening slumber causing many of them to prematurely deliver eggs and the family donkey suddenly made a noise that left him actually thinking he had been changed into a horse.

The real issue centered on two inescapable facts. First, Missy appeared at the window with a look on her face that resembled the look on Braveheart's face moments before he went into battle against the hated English invaders.

Second, mother and father. The expression on mother's face could well be explained with enough apologies and "didn't really mean it" and "came to defend sister's honor from the obvious onslaught of an enemy attack in the persons of Big Red and Lizard". Reputations to the rescue.

But one look at father's face, let alone the shotgun he was brandishing told an entirely different story. Watch out! His demeanor was a mixture between a cross-eyed bull-dog just cheated out of the last bite of the lamb bone given to him personally by the master of the house, and a wild-eyed hyena licking his chops at the discovery of the putrid remains of a rotting corpse under the African sun.

Even at the age of seventy-nine the aftermath of this unfortunate adventure into puberty could well be felt and remembered.

Four

Then there was the church. His folks were religious indeed. All the folks in their corner of Texas were religious. Just wasn't patriotic not to be. Sunday was the Lord's Day. Everything was laid aside. Missy spent the better part of Saturday laying out her clothes but always said the same thing every Sunday morning.

"I don't know what I am going to wear!"

Albright heard it so often he would actually mouth the words in full and unapologetic view of the entire family at the exact moment she said it. Then, every item of clothing had to match. Albright had never heard anything so stupid. At any rate you couldn't see that bra-thing anyway and so who cared what matched if you couldn't see the only thing that really mattered.

And the same was true concerning Nesty. Had his eyes on her since they were little and saw the same things appearing on her as on Missy. Fascinating! Just fascinating.

He dreaded Sundays except for the opportunity to see Nesty up close and personal. Everybody was solemn. What really puzzled him was the way everyone was so sweet all of a sudden. Even Big Red smiled, especially when the reverend asked him to do something. He suddenly got polite. Those church days were something else. Long and drawn out. Not a complaint out loud to be heard. Not even by Mrs. Goshbottom who could be heard from miles away telling her unfortunate husband, Mr. Goshbottom, just how sorry he was. Albright once saw him being beaten up with Mrs. Goshbottom's broom stick to the point at which he cowered in the corner with an arm raised over his head pledging fresh allegiance to the flag of the United Sates of America and to the "wife of his bosom," Mrs. Edwina Goshbottom.

The offense, apparently, was his utter and complete failure to pick enough green beans for the green bean casserole. The ladies of the weekly ladies' Bible study group would be deeply offended at the sight of such a diminutive looking green bean casserole and this would reflect directly on Mrs. Goshbottom's character.

As always, Mr. Goshbottom was seated right in front of his wife who was in the second row behind the deacons. Her seat was part of the guarantee of the church. In fact she had to sit there so as to be able to give Mr. Goshbottom the instructions necessary to carry out his important role as an officer of the church. Her looks made it certain he was duly elected every three years, even though there had been no change in the deacons for the last couple or three decades. It seemed as though deacons were deacons for all time and eternity. It was rumored Mister Henry Fortenberry had been a deacon for over one hundred years, which explained why he had to go to the toilet at the same time every Sunday, in the exact middle of the reverend's sermon. The toilets were directly outside the door to the left of the choir loft and pulpit but no one dared to even giggle when Mister Fortenberry went in there in the middle of the sermon. It was obvious his wife was dead because whatever it was he ate for breakfast every Sunday did not take too kindly to being cooped up in Mister Fortenberry's stomach.

It sounded like a hundred chickens were being plucked alive at the same time. But the straw that broke the camel's back was when Mister Fortenberry emerged from one of his mid-sermon trips with toilet paper trailing in a long line behind him, all the way back to his seat on the fourth row. He must have owned that seat or something because if anyone else sat there they got glared at until they up and moved.

And what was really strange was most of the deacons were not what they were on Sundays. In fact Albright had been severely reprimanded by his mother and father for just mentioning the fact that Deacon Thompson could cuss as well as Deacon Bandy. The two of them had gotten into it at Deacon Thompson's 'cash only' car wash that was meant to wash cars clean but always left stuff behind. As he recalled, this is what had happened. Supporting Deacon Thompson's business was one thing. But the whole purpose for paying all that cash money, up front, was to "get rid of all them bugs and stuff." Only when Deacon Badly said "bugs and stuff" he scowled so deep you could run irrigation pipes through the furrows on his brow. His Texas accent took the "u" in "bugs and stuff" and dropped the bottom part of the "u" into the lower parts of his bowels. The sound it produced was a mixture between a serious bowel movement Albright had heard coming from his own father, and a bull frog trying to croak with a bad case of throat infection.

In hindsight, from the perspective of his seventy-nine years, Mister Rhodes could only shake his head. It certainly felt good to know he was the youngest elected deacon of the church.

Five

The church had played a very important part in his success story. He knew this deep down in his heart. Of course "serving the Lord" was what was always said, especially at church functions. And he loved to hear the reverend remark just how wonderful it was to have all the members of the congregation, and especially the deacons "serving the Lord with all their heart and soul and mind."

Looking at the reverend reminded Albright and his entire cast of fellow Sunday morning sufferers of the pain one would expect to see on a "love-bug's" face just moments before it ran head long into the windshield of a Ford truck. It was hard to describe and very difficult to imagine. Add a few sour grapes forced into his mouth and then observe the black robe drawn over his shoulders with ketchup stains permanently etched into the fabric, and you've got the picture. This man was unsmiling, unfriendly, excepting when the grandparents were around, and mean as a boa-constrictor. To make matters worse he obviously didn't wear a watch and Albright could well remember what seemed like his whole life going by one Sunday at a time. He also spat. Real bad when he was sounding out on hell and all the brimstones and "you are obviously going there, boy" sermons. And this all over a small piece of chewing gum smuggled in during Sunday School.

One time, Big Red dispatched Lizard to deposit a few pieces of already well chewed gum right under the pew within

easy reach of Big Red's chubby fingers. This had to be done under the guise of "needing to go" in the middle of the Sunday
School lesson which was probably on the lump of salt that was
that fellow's wife because she behaved just like "them boys"
behaved. To Lizard this command rivaled the "Great Commission" thing some woman whose name was something with a
moon in it, had invented.

Anyway, back to the reverend. Baptisms were his favorite
thing to do. It was apparent to Albright that "dunking" was
important because of all the "amens" that accompanied each
one. The reverend literally threw himself into this thing and it
was not uncommon to have to have the emergency people
standing in wait to apply the "breathing thing" when the reverend got carried away. He would scowl at the repentant sinner and then hold up one hand like he was imagining himself
to be Moses parting the Red Sea. Then in a sing-song kind of
booming voice he would recite something about fathers and
sons and spirits which was designed to make the whole family feel good about being included in this thing. Then he
would step forward and throw the unfortunate victim down
under the water with such gusto a wave of water would rise
up on the other side and look like the pictures Albright had
seen of the Galveston coast line after a hurricane had done its
dirty work.

Sadly, however, the backward "swish" of the water recoil-
ing off the back wall would pass over the head of the just
emerging sinner, catch the forward wall, and then return just in
time to slam a few gallons right up the nostrils of the one who
had just began to take a big breath of air.

The church organist was always most displeased. Even
though she was very large and needed a refreshing shower on
those steamy summer evenings, she would stand up with her
hands on her hips and reveal a soaked upper garment that now
fully exposed an enormous set of equipment of sorts that comprised her undergarment. In full view of the entire membership she would latch one set of fingers under the right side of
her undergarment and the other set of fingers under the left
side. In one movement she would pull at both ends. There was
a wet suction kind of noise followed by a loud slapping smack

that sounded like a cannon being fired at point blank range into a wet blanket.

Baptism was very important to Albright. He "walked the aisle" during Vacation Bible School at the age of seven because he sure didn't want to go to hell. All his friends did too. It was kind of a fun thing to do together, anyway.

"Ain't going to that hot place," he announced in an effort to ward off the two Chester boys who got in his face and started to call him a sissy. "Besides you did too. Everyone's done that thing and you know it!"

At the age of seventy-nine he smiled with satisfaction because he had instructed his entire family to get baptized too. It was the proper thing to do, he said.

His own baptism was one for the books. Fortunately the church had enough sense to have Vacation Bible School in the summer time. This was good thinking because the thought of having a swim on a hot summer's evening was not entirely unpleasant. That's why most of his friends agreed to do it as well.

Problem was the church was small by the standards of Albright's large church in New Orleans. And they didn't have air-conditioning in those early days either.

He remembered how pleased his mother had been. So pleased she had called all her friends and had even agreed to invite Mrs. Darcy over for a good glass of seriously sweetened iced tea. This tea was made, prepared, bombarded with at least seventeen huge cups of Louisiana sugar, and then set out on the porch to draw. Any effort on the part of anyone, including the dogs and cats to touch the tea before the matron of the house declared it "just right" was considered a capital offense. Lizard came close one day and almost had his left hand amputated by an indignant mother.

Just five days before the troop of Vacation Bible School boys had plucked up the courage to walk down front, Mildred had denounced this same lady as Satan's closest friend. This was probably because her daughter, a tubby little thing, had been named to the county queen's court. Mrs. Rhodes regarded this as a further sign of witchcraft because Missy was head and shoulders prettier than Suzie. Besides Missy was an inch taller and had better diction, her mother opined.

Baptism provided an opportunity to engage in serious festivities. Occasionally one or two of the more religious-minded members would bring up the issue of salvation, and personal relationship, and the Lord Jesus Christ, but no one wanted to dampen the enthusiasm or spoil the fun. To the best of Albright's memory the church on that day was packed to capacity. The small baptismal pool had been exposed from under the pulpit, which had been carefully carried out into the adjoining classroom. This classroom also served as the reverend's study, and no boy ever wanted to be summonsed into that dark place.

The large number who had surrendered their lives and requested baptism meant the church had an unusual problem. There was no where to dress and undress for the event. The candidates had been instructed to bring white clothing with something to change into for the church-wide reception to follow on the grounds. Mrs. Simmons had reluctantly volunteered to bake one of her renowned chocolate cakes, even though everyone knew her husband would eat most of it before it was laid on the table. He was very fat and loved chocolate cake.

In order to overcome the problem a deacon's meeting was called to order by the chairman. This was a matter of grave urgency and involved at least a three hour heated discussion by all five deacons. The decision was made to hang two curtains; one from the baptistry to the wall on the left side of the church facing the congregation, and the other in like manner on the right hand side. A make-shift pole, mounted in a bucket of concrete, was to be the pillar of strength. This special and generous gift was given by Mister Nimbo whose father had been a founding member of the church.

Archibald Nimbo looked just like his late father, they all said, and even carried the rather large black mole above his top lip with the big black hairs coming out of it, just like his father.

Anyway, Albright could still picture the scene.

"Remember that circus, Nesty?" he queried from the comfort of his personally designed seat on his private jet as they flew across the Atlantic.

"What circus, Albright?" the lady of the house replied without looking up from her knitting needles. The sweater she was knitting for her grandson was almost complete.

"Back in Texas when the old reverend dunked me and that whole bunch of savages," he explained with a kind of muffled laugh often heard by distinguished men who want to bust their sides in sheer laughter and yet are contained by the need to remain somewhat composed and dignified due to their station in life.

With the female side of the "change room" jam-packed the reverend entered the water and gestured for the first lady to enter by using the make-shift steps which had been built by none other than Mister Jackson himself. No one in the county had a better reputation for sturdiness in construction than Mister Jackson. It was rumored one of the Governors of Texas had his own private pool "stepped" by Mister Jackson.

Shockingly the first lady to walk the steps was Mrs. Gushkin. To say she was large would have been the understatement of the century, let alone of the year. Big Red reported hearing his father say that if Mrs. Gushkin ever rode one of his fine Clydesdales she would snap its back instantly. It looked like her neck, chest and stomach were one and the same thing. What puzzled all the children was how she ever went places. Her stomach seemed to overlap in a critical fashion down to her knees, but many a young person swore she had no knees either.

The worst scenario, however, was related to her very loving disposition. She picked on the boys and loved to draw them to herself and envelop them in her arms. Many a young boy was literally left gasping for air. Some were even heard making vows of celibacy, if this is what it meant to be married.

As Mrs. Gushkin lowered herself down the steps into the baptismal pool the water began to rise. Much to the shock of the congregation it actually rose so high that it was teetering on the lip of the pool just as the reverend raised his hand to announce the inclusion of the lady's father, son and a deceased member of her family, who went by the name of "halle spirit". He never left family out.

Afterwards, some claimed that they detected a slight trace of panic in her eyes just moments before her backward plunge into the water. The reverend never looked more determined to demonstrate his God-given strength than in this time of need.

As he pushed her backwards and down a number of things happened simultaneously. The water rose at an alarming rate and began to gush over the edge of the pool. Even those choir members who had moved to the front row next to the deacons were drenched. Sensing her imminent demise, Mrs. Gushkin drew on all her means of resistance. For a split second she knew she was drowning and, with one look at the reverend's face, knew he was the enemy. Her left hand went up and began to circle around trying to find something to hold on to. By now the back part of her large stomach had made contact with the floor of the baptistry, had bounced off the floor and had caught up with the front part of her stomach. Underwater it must have looked like the huge blob of something ricocheting off a concrete wall and going in the opposite direction. The momentum helped her left hand to find focus. She groped and thrashed about until, by sheer accident, she suddenly found something to hold on to.

Problem was it was the top part of the curtain that connected both the men's and ladies' change rooms. With a sudden swoosh, and much to the dismay of the reverend who was now trying to extract his own head from the water where he, too, had been immersed, the entire contraption began to fall down.

Over on the men's side Mr Nesbit had just completely undressed and was facing the congregation, totally "in the buff." As was the tradition in the church the ladies of the Women's Missionary Union were seated in their usual place on the right front row as a complement to the deacons. Their gasps and cries for help, let alone the look on Mr Nesbit's face would never be forgotten.

Of course Albright saw immediately the value of a pool of water like the one he had been baptized in. One time, he remembered, the heat of summer was stifling. Baptism was scheduled for the evening. So the boys gathered together and determined a swim in the pool would carry the day. At about two o'clock on Sunday afternoon, Albright, Big Red, Lizard, Buzzard, whose real name was Billy, and Snake, whose real name was Shaun, harnessed their swimming stuff and crept into the church.

What a time they had together. The old pulpit made an excellent diving board while the front pew provided a good run off point. Albright brought along the new goggles and snorkels he had been given for his eighth birthday with a trip to the beach at Galveston in mind. Lizard had collected a few extra dimes and cents. They made terrific objects to dive for. In the heat of their enjoyment Albright came up for air to discover to presence of the chairman of the diaconate who had come in just to check the level of the water for the baptism that evening.

It was amazing how quickly they cleaned the place up and just how quiet and well behaved they were in church and Sunday School for many months to follow. The fact the chairman never reported the incident either to his father or the reverend really helped the youngster to appreciate the role and the solemn responsibilities of the church deacon. He remembered this later in life when his turn came around, in New Orleans, where the family estate was located.

Six

A lbright grimaced in pain again. His wife said something about Monaco and he was glad for the distraction. The Italian Riviera had been their favorite destination for many years. At least he could gamble and have some serious fun there without having to feel guilty when he came up for deacon election at their big church in New Orleans. There were things about him that were his private business, anyway. He ordered another cup of his favorite herbal tea. The raspberry flavor soothed his throat and seemed to help him breathe properly. Deep down he knew something was seriously wrong with him. Perhaps they should have listened to the specialist and just stayed at home in the Garden district.

He would always be glad his father had made those business trips to New Orleans in the early days. It had something to do with the cattle, he thought. Albright was glad of that even though he remembered the terrible fight his father and mother had gotten into one time after he returned from the big city on the Mississippi River. All he heard was his mother crying and screaming.

"How could you do this to me and the children?" She pounded the seat and pulled down on her long black hair as though trying to tear every strand out of her head. "You ever go back to that Oyster Bar I'll take the kids and leave you!" she shouted hysterically.

His father sounded really sorry and remorseful and said something about "a mistake" and "it just happened" and "indiscretion," but whatever it was the years managed to erase it. Only once in a while his mother would storm out of the house saying something about "you'll never go back there to that slut as long as I live" or "I've got a good mind to tell the reverend," but nothing much ever came of it.

Ernestine Rothschild was as "cute as a button" from the day he first laid eyes on her. Her daddy doted on her and called her "my cute little Nesty". It was at the church dinner-on-the-ground when he was just twelve or so when they met for the first time. Her parents had obviously made it big. You could tell it by the new outfits she always wore, and besides everybody knew it. They also drove a new Ford and had lots of picnics and stuff over at their farm.

Mister Rothschild came from the Rothschild family which included some of the largest cattle barons north of the Rio Grande. He also was a full partner in the company that produced the best selling hot sauce, called Texas Mete. Everybody had at least three or four bottles of Texas Mete on the table at every meal because everybody knew you couldn't call yourself a real Texan if you didn't have Texas Mete. A meal just wasn't a meal without it. It was the real "Meat" of Texas.

Albright heard his daddy remark, more than once, that if he had just a fraction of the Rothschild fortune he would retire and move to Austin to set up his own barbeque business.

He watched her every move and even seriously considered a contract murder when that miserable boy, Roy Sandringham, tried to make a move on Nesty. She was so pretty. She had long blonde hair, with eyes that seemed to sparkle in the sun. When she ran it was like watching grace in motion and when she sang it was like listening to a whole choir of angels. Albright did everything possible to get her attention all the way through middle and junior high school. But to no avail. She was a rich kid and people like Albright were just a step below the family expectation. Besides her mother and father protected her like a lioness does her pride of cubs. She was going to marry well, or not at all.

As luck would have it, Albright excelled at sports. In his junior year he was selected to play football for the varsity squad. By the time he graduated, cum laude, he had been selected to the All State Team and was also the MVP of the All

Star game in Houston. Word had it that were it not for his size he would have probably been drafted as a professional.

The "full ride" to play ball at Baylor was hardly unexpected. Before heading to Tulane for Law School he tried out for the Bucs and the Saints but was cut both times.

Fortunately all of this caught the eye of a certain cheerleader by the name of Ernestine Rothschild. The first date they had followed much scheming on his part, especially the meeting "by accident" at her seventeenth birthday bash out at Child's Play, the family estate.

Mr. Rothschild was not charmed in the least when he noticed his little girl blushing under the steady gaze of this boy from the small holding down the road. Admittedly things did change a bit when the company struck a small, but profitable oil well on the Rhodes' property. It guaranteed an extra four grand a month, which was a lot of money back then. The initiation he had to go through for Ernestine's debutante ball stretched him a bit, he would admit later. But by then the stupidity of the Big Reds and the disdain for the likes of Lizard and company had become the order of the day. It was obvious those types were never going to make anything of themselves. They would end up selling hamburgers or delivering pizzas or something else. They never applied themselves and increasingly dropped to levels far below the lofty ideals firmly embedded in the mind of Albright A. Rhodes.

The Baylor days were filled with football, fraternities and Ernestine. His rise to prominence was rapid and secure. After all, he was a star football player and had a Rothschild on his arm. He was always careful to play the right part for the right occasion. Social esteem was very important. Conduct becoming a man of his intellect and stature was uppermost in his mind. Ernestine hung on to him with a glow of pride and loved to parade her fine catch just as much as he did. Trips back to Child's Play became more and more frequent as her father doted on his lovely daughter and her handsome boyfriend.

On very select occasions they would venture back to church. The one back home, that is. It was a little costly in terms of their reputation but Christmas and Easter were always a good excuse to go. The old reverend had died of a massive heart attack and the new preacher-boy was fresh behind the ears. He had to be checked out carefully by a select few of the men who kind of ran things around there. The young pastor and his wife spent an entire week being taken, one at a time, to each one of these people's homes or businesses, depending on which of these was the more convenient. Apparently he passed the test. His trial sermon went well.

Seven

Once he arrived at Baylor there was really little time for church. He had so much to do, so many responsibilities as a leader. And all the social functions fell quite naturally in line. Once or twice he would get slightly "tipsy" after having a few too many. But, on the whole, Albright stuck to social drinking. He was a good man. When elected into one of many leadership positions he carried out his responsibilities with great determination. He was never derelict in his duty. Everyone, including his professors, admired him and he began to be held up as a model of excellence.

In his sophomore year his father died after a short illness. He immediately saw to it that his mother was well taken care of in the retirement home. The farm sold for over three hundred thousand and money was not the issue. There were also the rights to the oil well which brought in a lifetime packet for her. Missy, unfortunately, went and got pregnant. She married the fellow but soon suffered horrible abuse.

Albright was glad he was able to buy his sister and her new husband a small house in the Gentilly suburb of New Orleans. Eventually, he would give them some small responsibility looking after a segment of the Texas Mete industry he would inherit from Mister Rothschild.

When the New Orleans Saints decided against drafting Albright he turned his attention to more important things. First there was the matter of marriage. In secret he went to Mister Rothschild at the most appropriate time.

Sunday afternoon at the tennis club was perfect, especially if Landrum H. Rothschild had been successful and had won his game of doubles. He and Dr. George C. Wiley had been tennis partners for years and had all the trophies to prove it. Needless to say, few of the others would want to be known as the ones who beat the owner of Texas Mete and the most famous cardiologist in the country. Besides, hunting trips to Mexico and even to Africa were on the line.

Albright ordered another cold Budweiser from the personal steward on his plane and remembered that day so well. "How are you going to take care of her, boy?" and, "what, exactly do you plan to do with your life?" and, "it takes money you know, lots of it!"

"Besides," he went on with somewhat of a glint in his eye, "how can I be sure you'll keep your money in your pocket and keep your pants on too?"

Nesty's father would love to say that while stealing a glance at the girl's mother. With Ernestine being the only child, Albright had an inkling where the money would come from. But he loved this girl and that was all that mattered.

The Rothschild's were Christians, of course. Both were life-long members of the church and both had been baptized. In fact it was only after the new preacher had begun his ministry at the church that the family had felt "forced" to leave. He had a little too much enthusiasm for their liking and wanted to change some things, like the way the deacons were elected. Landrum had been asked almost every year to allow his name to "go forward" as a deacon but he always declined saying he was too busy. Besides he understood how important his money was, especially for the things he thought needed attention in the church. At any rate being a deacon would interfere with his ability to dispense the money properly.

The "straw that broke the camels' back" was the young preacher's insistence that people make it a matter of public record that they had "given their hearts and lives to Jesus." This really annoyed Mister Rothschild. He believed this whole matter was a private thing between a person and God. It was nobody else's business. There was nothing worse than a fanatic, he would say. So he and the family moved their membership to another church where privacy was respected and at least they could go to the club immediately after the sermon was concluded. That young "buck" would always insist on making the entire congregation stand and sing while he begged and begged for people to "turn their lives over to Jesus". It was all too much, really!

The wedding, itself, was a spectacular affair. Obviously the church was too small so the entire day was out at Child's Play. Elaborate and extravagant were the hallmarks of their nuptials. Albright's mother wept through the whole thing. The premarital counseling the preacher required them to go through was tolerated at the most. Albright hardly listened to a word he was saying. All he could think about was his beautiful bride to be. Besides all the talk about "keeping Jesus at the center of your life and marriage" was obvious stuff. The real issues were their impending move to New Orleans and Tulane School of Law and the setting up of their new home. They had a standard to maintain, after all. And, of course, he couldn't wait to get her into that bedroom.

His father-in-law had recently made the decision to move the company to New Orleans. The market potential was better and he also felt he could ride the coattails of his arch rival Tabasco which was part of the Cajun mystic. It was manufactured on Avery Island just near Lafayette, Louisiana. Texas Mete had distribution centers in nearly every major city in North America but was still dwarfed by Tabasco.

The overseas market was on the rise without a doubt. The year Albright and his bride married, Texas Mete opened markets in Australia, New Zealand, South Africa and the United Kingdom, Italy and France. Mister Rothschild was launching a new campaign to capitalize on the Texas mystic overseas. "The Real Texas Mete" began to appear on billboards and advertisements all around the world. Texas and America were synonymous to millions of people overseas.

Luck was on the march, Albright was convinced. Fate was at work and he was obviously the chosen one.

Eight

Billy Bob was actually born William Terence Malkmus, the third, eighty-nine years before he noticed the sores on his right hand. His mother said he was named for his grandfather, William Terence Malkmus. Her father had been the man whose name would appear many years later in the same book with some of the other jazz greats like Louis Armstrong and B. B. King. Apparently he could play the piano as well as anyone in New Orleans. Someone said Louis remarked on more than one occasion that Willy could "tinkle those ivories" and set up a beat as well as the best, especially when they played together at Preservation Hall in the French Quarter. That's how he made his living, his daughter would tell her son. Willy would simply put his hat down wherever he was playing. People would come by and just drop a few bucks in the hat if they felt like it. The best place to play was just around Jackson Square, and especially in front of the Cathedral. They were convinced the Spirit of the Lord was there. Or at least one of His Angels.

Willy began early in the morning sometimes and usually washed his gumbo down with gallons of iced tea. Every now and then they would ask him to play for a jazz funeral. He loved those particularly because they paid him something anyway. The procession would start real slow and then would break into real fast and hard beat jazz. You would think the dead person was being celebrated. The tourists loved these things and were always real generous. Sometimes rich folks would just hire them to do a jazz funeral and put on a show for guests who had come from as far away as California.

Willy had to play the accordion because a piano was too heavy to wheel down the pot-holed roads of the Quarter. They would always end up at one of the cemeteries which looked real different in New Orleans because everybody was buried above the ground in a mausoleum looking tomb. Billy Bob's mother said it was because New Orleans was something like five feet below sea level. That always bothered the young Billy Bob because his mother would get mad at him and call him "something below five foot" and take a swipe at him. One day he knew a hurricane would come and wipe out the whole city.

Nine

Billy didn't have a father. His mother said she was raped one night between the French Market and the Mississippi River. It was late and she was heading back to her shot-gun home just near the highway that wound its way right over Canal Street. She didn't bother to report it to the police because she knew they would just look at her and some of them would even smile and pass ugly comments. Besides she had been with a number of different men over the years to try and get security and shelter and things. When her daddy had died of a stroke she was only thirteen years old and had no one to care for her. She spent her days scrounging for food and then taking odd jobs doing all kinds of things. Her favorite job was when she worked at Masperos right there near the river. There was a brewery over the road but the food was the big attraction. Even back then, people would line up outside in the street just to get a seat and eat a mufalata. The other favorite went by the name of "po-boy" which was short for "poor boy". This was a sort of long sandwich on which you could have shrimp, or oysters, or cat-fish and then cover it all over with hot sauce. The folks who came to Masperos drank lots of beer, made a lot of noise and gave great tips to people like Billy Bob's mother. She knew how to work a table.

Her life changed, she said, when she had nowhere to have this baby. A friend told her about a place called by the name of Brantley or something where people would help people like her. And so that's where William Terence Malkmus, the third, was born. He still couldn't figure out what happened to William Terence Malkmus the second.

Every time Billy Bob recalled the story of his birth a smile would break out on his old, wrinkled and pain-ridden face. Lying there in the servants' quarters of the Rhodes' estate just off St. Charles Avenue he thought deeply and with much inner satisfaction of those early days.

Perhaps what meant more to him than anything else was the way in which his mother's life had been changed. Until he reached the age of seven their life had been a literal hell on earth. No where to go, nowhere to sleep, nothing much to eat. The men who hung around his mother did strange and cruel things to her. Sometimes he would be curled up in the back seat of a parked car when the men would arrive and do things to her. Sometimes he had to go to dives and hovels under bridges and by-passes. He clearly remembered the time when he had to see his mother dragged off to prison by the New Orleans Police Department. She was crying.

Then there was the time when she got this job on Bourbon Street and had to take all her clothes off and dance and stuff and keep kissing this silver pole she had to hold on to. Then she started drinking real bad. It started with just a little wine or beer here and there. But after a while she had to have more. It was like medicine to her, she said. That's when they would sleep on a bench right on the banks of the river until some cop would come and tell them to move on or else.

But then it all changed.

Ten

His mother was walking down one of the side streets in the French Quarter one day when she was approached by three nice looking young students. They said they were from the seminary on Washington Avenue in the Garden District. It was the one near Commander's Palace where all the locals would go for the "Blue Plate" specials. Apparently they had some really good news to share with her. They asked if she went to church anywhere and she said, "of course not!" One of them began to tell her about the Lord Jesus Christ. A black covered book appeared from one of the students' back packs. He opened it up and flipped the pages to something he wanted to read to Billy Bob's mother.

"For God so loved the world He gave His only begotten Son, that whosoever believeth in Him should not perish but have everlasting life."

They told her something she had never heard before. God loved her. Jesus died on a cross for her. They also said Jesus knows all about her and even knows her by name. That just blew his mother out of the water. She didn't want to hear any more but just couldn't stop listening. She told them she had to go but promised to meet them again a few days later. Of course she had no intention of doing so but when the day and hour came she just felt herself drawn back to where the three students were waiting.

They were so kind and one of them even took young Billy Bob over the road to a burger joint and bought him a double hamburger with double cheese and french fries and a chocolate milkshake as well. His mother was crying real bad when he returned. Before they left they invited both Billy and his mother to a meeting of people they called a revival. It was going on at a church on Elysian Fields Avenue not far from where the seminary had moved to in later years, just around the corner from Gentilly Boulevard.

That same night his mother gave Billy Bob a bath in a tub of water for the first time in memory. She even brushed his hair and tried to look decent herself. She only had one dress which was torn on the left side and had pieces of cotton and stuff hanging from all the joints and connections. She even found an old clip to hold back the one side of her hair. Even at the age of eighty-nine Billy Bob could recall how pretty he thought his Mamma was that evening. He had never seen her so dolled up!

They walked all the way from the Gumbo Shop, on the corner of Iberville and Rampart, where she washed dishes, to the church where they said there was a special place reserved for the two of them. Panic almost set in when they arrived. There were lots of people already in the church. Some real friendly people wanted to shake their hands and a tall man in a dark suit escorted them into the church and told them they could sit in a place reserved for special people like them. Billy could never remember anyone calling him or his Mama special.

Everybody stood up and sang songs. Then a young woman got up and told everyone just how much Jesus had changed her life. Then they all sang again. When they handed a plate around for money his mother didn't know where to look because she didn't have any money. But no one seemed to care if she put anything in the plate or not. They just kept on talking about Jesus all the time.

Then another lady stood up pulled out a dummy toy that went by the name of Bennie. She and Bennie had this talk going and Bennie even talked about Jesus and made everyone laugh. Billy Bob really thought that was the stuff. He had never seen anything like it before. Finally this man stood up behind this bench thing and began to shout and make gestures. Billy's mother whispered in his ear that this man was called the preacher. Billy at first thought he was angry but then saw the smile on his face. He told them all about sin. He said it was like a whole lot of ugly stuff that people do. Like lying and things. It reminded Billy of an incident that happened to him.

Eleven

Billy Bob knew the preacher was right because just the day before he and his best friend, Boudreaux, had cornered Mamie Wendelheaver's black cat and had scared the living daylights out of him. They had to do something to get back at her because she was always mean to them. She swore at his mother every time they crawled back into the space behind the kitchen where he and his Mama had set up home. At least they had somewhere to sleep and lots of garbage cans to scrounge for scraps of food left by all those rich folks who always had more on their plates than six people could eat, let alone one. He and Boudreaux, who came from just south of New Orleans, from a place called Cut Off in the Bayou, took hold of the opportunity when they saw Mamie Wendelheaver head out with an old grocery cart she had evidently borrowed from the store the last time she went shopping. Whenever she was pushing that thing they knew she would be gone all day because she always came back late at night with all kinds of junk stuff in the grocery cart. And none of it was groceries. She even brought back an old hub-cap one time and used it to decorate her part of the space.

Any rate Billy and Boudreaux had planned this a long time. They even sketched some drawings on a piece of brown paper they had stolen from Jego. Jego was the old bum who lived on the bench opposite the police station in the French Quarter. He told the boys the police had asked him to station himself there as a kind of secret protection service in case there was trouble for the police. He had been an FBI agent, at one time, he said. He spent the better part of his busy days picking up thrown down unsmoked cigarettes. He would break them open and collect all the unburned tobacco. Then he would get his piece of brown paper and roll all the unsmoked tobacco in it and light it. Sometimes it would kind of catch fire and he would cough so deep you would think a freight train was passing by.

Billy Bob remembered the day he and Boudreaux had found Jego dead. He looked like he had fallen in the gutter and smashed his head on the statue. Green stuff was hanging out of his nose and roaches, the size of big lizards were crawling in his eyes and mouth. A truck stopped and picked him up and drove off.

So, they caught the black cat. Being near July fourth the boys had collected a few of those fire crackers that go off in sequence and sound like a roll of thunder stretching from the Texas panhandle to the Florida Keys.

At eighty-nine Billy Bob could only chuckle as he pictured what happened to Mamie's beloved cat.

With Boudreaux holding on to its mouth to stop it from biting Billy tied a whole bunch of these thunder crackers to the tail of the victim. One match was all it took. The last they remember seeing of the dreaded feline was what appeared to be thunderous succession of booms and flashes and sparks accompanied by a black blur somewhat reminiscent of Donald Campbell breaking the land speed record in his blue-bird.

Suddenly the preacher raised his voice again and Billy's thoughts came back into the revival service where he was sitting next to his mother.

Twelve

What surprised Billy and his mother was that the preacher told them all people have sin. He went on to explain that Jesus died on a cross for all people. Then, suddenly, this preacher told them if they wanted to give their hearts to Jesus they would need to come down to the front and take him by the hand. Before he knew it his mother was out there and down front without even saying good morning to Billy. There she was on her knees and there was this lady with arms all around her and they were praying and saying things out loud to God.

Thirteen

Billy Bob had stood in Jackson Square many a time and watched a whole parade of people with all kinds of purple and gold necklaces and things doing things like this. He didn't know anything about religion and religious people—even when those religious people were important. On one occasion Billy just happened to be in the right place when the chief one came from Italy. Billy stood there watching and remembered you could hardly see him going down Canal Street there were so many people and police. The religious man was being driven in a vehicle that looked to Billy like a white kind of golf cart looking car that drove him down the road as he waved to everybody. Some of the other religious people who were dressed up in fancy outfits were waving smoke in pots at everybody. Billy and Boudreaux tried to figure out why it was they were waving smoke pots at the people. Boudreaux suggested it was to help kill all the mosquitoes in Louisiana. It seemed everywhere they went they had to deal with huge mosquitoes. He had heard them called the state bird of Louisiana, but he didn't believe that. He'd seen birds a lot bigger when he and Boudreaux sneaked into the Audubon Zoo.

They had crawled through the opening in the fence that ran along the Mississippi River where the boat brought the people from the wharf at the Quarter. Billy Bob had no money to do stuff like that and spent many hours standing there watching people come and go in and out of the Zoo. He would see all the little boys and girls hopping around and skipping with excitement. Most of them had huge ice-creams in cones. He always wondered what it would be like to go into that Zoo with a huge chocolate ice cream just hanging over the edges.

Sometimes he would see one of those big ones just fall out of the cone on the street. Often the kid would kick up such a fuss and throw things and shout at his Mama and she would pat him on the head and say she was sorry on behalf of the fallen ice cream. Then she would go and get him another. That's when Billy Bob would move in and pick up the fallen ice cream. It would be filled with dirt and little stones and stuff but he didn't mind. He was used to eating scraps of food that had fallen from rich people's tables.

Fourteen

When his mother finally stood up she had a smile on her face that Billy Bob would never forget for the rest of his life. The preacher put his arm around her and said she had given her heart and life to Jesus Christ. The whole crowd of people clapped their hands and looked real happy except for the man who sat a short way from Billy whose wife cried the whole time the other fellow was talking and shouting. He sort of didn't look like he wanted to be there and was real mad the whole time. Billy studied him real hard because he was familiar.

Then he remembered where it was he'd seen the man. It was the day before at Café du Monde where those delicious cake things covered with white powder were served. Billy knew all about them because he and Boudreaux and the others often found stacks of them in the garbage cans in the alley between the café and the wall. They had to share them with the cats and roaches but Billy didn't mind. They were unreal and he and the others would blow powder on each other and have a good laugh.

Anyway this same man, he remembered, was drinking coffee with lots of milk boiled in it and had a stack of those cake things and was having such a good time. One of the old horn players from the Quarter came up to the sidewalk and started playing real good music. This man loved it. He clapped with the rhythm and even got up and put some money in the man's hat to say thank you.

But not when he came to church. No sir, he wasn't a happy camper. He wouldn't clap or even sing and sat there with his arms folded like he was real mad the whole time church was on. It looked sort of strange to Billy Bob especially seeing everyone else was so happy and all that. And when they handed around a small plate thing for people to put money in this man looked even madder.

From that day on the most important thing, it seemed, to Billy Bob's mother, was to go to that church on Elysian Fields. It seemed like nothing else really mattered to her anymore. The thing Billy liked about it was how happy it made his mother. Before she had done a lot of crying. Some days she had done nothing but cry all the time. Billy remembered how sad that made him feel because he truly loved his mother. She always apologized for not having good food to eat and having to live in the space and walk all the way from the gumbo shop to church every time. But after she gave her life to Jesus it didn't matter to Billy Bob anymore. She was happy all the time even though they had nothing. Billy didn't even know they had nothing because he had always had nothing.

From the time his mother became a Christian she began to ask her son to do the same. She wanted her son to give his heart to Jesus real bad. To Billy it seemed like that was all his mother would talk about. She told him all about forgiveness of sin and that this Jesus was the one who paid the price for the sin of the world. One thing Billy Bob understood was about price paying. What happened in his life over the next few years taught him a lot about having to pay up for the wrong things he would do with Boudreaux and his friends.

Fifteen

Boudreaux was already in the prison for juveniles just near the Xavier University. The judge said he had to be taught a lesson especially seeing this was the sixth time he'd been caught for stealing. Billy Bob was just lucky to have escaped, and, seeing they were blood brothers there was no way Boudreaux would have turned him in.

It happened the night they sat in the little park after they had stolen some of the food from the French Market. Billy threw the stones at the old lady to distract her while Boudreaux loaded up on fruit and real good bread for po-boys. As they sat and ate both the boys took knives and cut themselves in the palm of their hands. Then they slapped their hands together and made a blood vow to always be brothers and never blurt on the other if one of them was ever caught. They had watched all the voodoo stuff many times in the Quarter. Billy knew it worked especially if you took pins and things and jabbed stuffed dolls in the behind it would make the person you chose to jump, jump!

Like the one time they all went down to the other side of Galliano near Point A La Hache in the bayou. Lil' Pink, which was his Mamas' way of saying Llewellyn for short, helped them to steal his neighbor's pirot. A pirot is a small canoe type boat that is common down there in the bayou. Pirot's are very hard to paddle—let alone stand up in. But the boys had grown up using them all their lives.

In the middle of the night they launched out to the place where Roach Guercio had carefully placed all his crab and shrimp nets. It was where the two currents of water met and was the best area for a big catch. They had to get him back. This was the law down there. Roach had sent two of his sons over to Big Pink's house. Big Pink was Lil' Pink's daddy who hated the Guercios and had been feuding with them for as long as they had all been born there. The two boys did a good job, especially when they crept into the chicken coop and plucked five of Pink's prize chickens without killing them. When Big Pink came home he found his chickens standing there naked and half dead. He made a vow to get them back.

The two brothers' names were Dwayne and P.J. They were the most notorious brothers on the Bayou and got up to all kinds of pranks. Problem was when they grew up a little their pranks turned into the kind of pranks the police got involved in. Dwayne especially was real mean and tough and no other boy liked to challenge his position on the Bayou. It was like he was sort of elected to the top spot on the Bayou without ever having to run in an election like the sheriff did, who had to put all kinds of billboards and notices in the ground on sticks.

One of the biggest events on the Bayou was when people had to vote to put other people in positions like the parish jurors or the sheriff and other officers. It was also a great time for social things. And so everybody was running around and talking and eating lots of crawfish and crabs.

At election time, these billboards and notices were all over the place. They had messages on them. Then, the one man would go on television and say the ugliest things about the other man who also wanted to get elected and he would even accuse him of running around on his wife and then the other one would say the one who said that didn't even know who his Mama was. One time they even had a fight right there on the steps of the mayor's office on Main Street. The one man's wife even started to punch the other man's wife and cuss and shout. Right there in front of all the children they said they were for and were going to take good care of if they were elected by the people who watched them fight on the steps. Then when they got elected they didn't do any of the things they said they would do like filling up all the pot-holes and making it easier to catch the turtles in the Bayou and more than one red-fish without a license and smaller than twenty-two inches. That made them all mad all the time because they said it was what they had to live on. So these men knew what would make these folks vote for them but when it happened they never did what they said they would do. So next time the fighting was even worse because the elected people always seemed to fall out of favor with the public who had elected them.

But not Dwayne. He occupied a special place of prominence in the Bayou community. It was even said that everybody knew Dwayne—and if they did not know him, they needed to get to know him because nobody messed with him. He never had to do all that stuff like go around and worry all the people when they were boiling their crawfish at night and knock on their doors and make some kind of promise. No, Dwayne just was in the top position. You could ask Edwin Crochet. He knew better than most of the folks and had a crooked nose, three broken ribs and a life-time of pain coupled with a permanent limp to prove his case. He said that was the last time he would ever even so much as look in the direction of one of Dwayne's girlfriends. If Dwayne had so much as smiled at one of them they were his for life. It was kind of the law down on the Bayou. A few of the boys had mysteriously turned up with alligator teeth marks on them because they just didn't get it.

And so the boys found themselves in a pirot heading towards the place where Roach Guercio had carefully placed all his crab and shrimp nets. Without so much as a thought the boys cut the nets to shreds and harvested a load of fresh crab and shrimp and even some oysters. They took them to the cabin and had a feast for three days before jumping a ride on an old truck back to New Orleans. On the way back they jabbed pins into a stuffed rhinoceros they found in a garbage dump near the Audubon Zoo. They figured Mister Guercio was a devil anyway and so the horn was just right even though there was only one. Down in New Orleans two horns meant bad. One horn was real bad. Like the special assistant to the devil himself.

Sixteen

Billy would, of course, never forget these experiences on the Bayou. Even as he lay dying many years later. Billy Bob grimaced in pain. The sharp stab of pain had seemed to move from his sores to the inside part of his body somehow. His wife reached over and patted him on the head like she always did when he was hurting.

"It'll be O.K., Sugar Lump," she would whisper in such a soft and tender way.

Billy wished he could reach over and hug her like he always did. She took a cold, damp cloth and mopped his sweating brow gently. Then, she stood up and walked past the T.V. and into the small, but adequate bathroom. To the outside observer it was a dive. But to them it was a palace. At least they had a roof over their heads, thanks to the kind generosity of Mister Rhodes.

The place itself was just off the outside patio at the back end of the mansion. A row of trees hid it from the eyes of passers by and the grand kids who loved to play ball and throw the Frisbee through the gap that led out onto the open field. The trees were essential but were never intended to prevent the children's access to the servants. When they called, any lapse of time was considered in a most serious light.

Like the time little Sonny had tripped and scuffed his knee. Mrs. Rhodes screamed for Billy Bob because she was convinced a tuft of uncut weed that had crept in one of the cracks in the concrete slab on the basketball court was the villain that caused little Sonny to trip. She was so mad that day you could see blue veins popping up in her neck.

"Just where do you think you have been you lazy oaf?" she barked at Billy Bob as he came running around the corner with his bad leg dragging behind him.

"Just when I need you, you are off loafing and playing the fool," she yelled. "Watch out! I've got a good mind to tell Mr. Rhodes. You can go back to your hovel on Bourbon Street."

Then, with a pause and sigh she said, "Just consider yourself lucky this time and on probation. What if my little Sonny had fallen and broken his arm or something, eh? What then?"

By then, of course, little Sonny, their four year old grandson, was already laughing and shooting at the little junior hoop Billy Bob had erected on the pole at the far end of the court. Sonny always seemed to get in the way of his fun.

Seventeen

Billy's wife of many years went by the name of Sue Ellen. She walked over to the basin and ran the hot water tap. Then she picked up another clean piece of that soft cloth and rinsed it out. Taking the basin she filled it up to the mark in the middle and walked back past the T.V. to where her husband lay stricken. He looked so frail and pitiful. A month before Mr. Rhodes had passed away, almost to the day, he had said he would send Billy to Oschner Hospital down off Jefferson Highway on the river. But since his death they had heard nothing more. When Sue Ellen brought up the subject Billy Bob would smile with that sweet gracious expression on his face.

"Don't worry Sweetness," he would say with a tenderness that would soothe a baby with sore gums.

"The family are still grieving. It's been so hard on them, you know. And, besides they are all down at the beach house in Orange Beach. When they get back next month perhaps you can talk to Mrs. Rhodes."

"Anyway, the Lord Jesus knows all about me. Let's not forget He has me in the palm of His hand. He's the great physician and if He wants me to get better I will. Now, Sweetness, I sure would appreciate it if you could help me roll over on my side. Those sores and things on my legs and back are killing me!"

She smiled.

As he lay there Billy's mind began to go back all those years again.

Eighteen

Dwayne and Billy Bob's lives had become intertwined. He recalled the day they met while Billy and Boudreaux were fishing under the big bridge that crossed over to Gretna on the West Bank. They became friends even though Dwayne lived most of the time down on the Bayou where his Dad was a shrimper. As things turned out both would end up in jail.

The way Dwayne got there would be no surprise to those who knew him. He crossed the line often and had no plans to turn around. There was a kind of hidden anger inside him. Besides he was tough and the undisputed leader of the Bayou. Both he and Billy Bob were headed in the same direction.

One day, when Dwayne was about sixteen, he and his buddies went after a group of guys who formed the official opposition. They waited in the shadows just outside the joint. Each one of them already had enough booze in them to make certain the plan would be followed through. It was so easy to get booze where they lived. Besides Frenchy was old enough and hung around with Dwayne as his kind of aide just so he could get his hands on some of the girls who hung around Dwayne. At the right time the signal was given and the boys moved in.

Once inside the baseball bats were put to work. The leader of the opposition didn't see it coming. The bat caught him full across the top of his nose. In slow motion it looked like his head began to burst open like a watermelon being belted with a big stick. First his nose separated just across the bridge. Then his eyes burst out of his head like a pimple being squeezed to the point at which the puss erupted from the ruptured head spewing its poison all over the place. He was unconscious before he hit the floor. Dwayne was arrested the next day just as he was preparing to move to Texas where his brother-in-law ran a small electrical business.

The police charged him with aggravated assault so long as the kid was still alive. If he died the charge would change to second degree murder. Of course no one could prove Dwayne was the one who swung the bat and his court-appointed lawyer was going to milk that one real good. In spite of this, Dwayne found himself transferred to the Juvenile prison in New Orleans.

There was many a day Billy would watch the kids playing in the school yard. The only education he had was a little his Mama had taught him. She had no money to send him to school and, besides, he had no decent clothes. The biggest problem was not being able to read. So he just pretended he could read and for the most part got away with it. He spent most of his days hunting for scraps of food and every now and then took some job which paid him next to nothing at all. And every time he had money he gave it to his mother. Most of it anyway!

Nineteen

It was while he washed dishes at the Oyster Bar that he first noticed Sue Ellen. Her Mama was one of the cooks at the Oyster Bar. She was really pretty and you could tell lots of the men thought she was fine. Apparently Sue Ellen never had a daddy that was anywhere around at least. So he and Sue Ellen had something in common. Billy soon found out her mama could even read. Some rich man had paid for her to learn how to read. He also sent her stuff every now and then, Sue Ellen told Billy. He had even given her a special painting of the river boats by some fellow to hang in her meager apartment at the back end of the Oyster Bar.

For days on end, if not months, Billy would track her every move. She was the most beautiful thing he had ever laid his eyes on. She had long black hair that seemed to curl around her chin in such a fashion as to make her look like she was one of the porcelain dolls Billy often stared at in the porcelain doll shop just near the place all the painters and self portrait artists sat with their boards. Billy spent many an hour with nothing else to do but sit and watch them at work. He wished he could draw like they could draw. Some of their pictures were real funny and made people laugh. Especially the little kids. He heard the Moms and Dads call those things "karikatures" or something but it didn't concern him too much because even if he did know what it was supposed to be he couldn't have spelled it anyway. So he would just sit there and laugh and smile with all the others. Sometimes Sue Ellen would sit with him. It became one of their favorite things to do.

One time he stole enough money to take her on a real date. They went to Café Du Monde and sat down on the real chairs and listened to the man who played the trombone with the crazy hat on. For the only time in his life Billy Bob stood up and walked over to him when he knew everybody was watching, especially Sue Ellen. He stopped in front of the man with the trombone. He was playing "When the Saints Go Marching In".

Billy knew that song because he had heard "Satchmo", which was Louis Armstrong's real name, sing that when he and Boudreaux and the others had climbed the fence early and had sat in the little opening behind Preservation Hall. Satchmo had this growling gruff sort of voice with a smile that looked like all the ivories on a piano when he smiled. Billy remembered how sad he felt when the old crooner died of heart trouble or something. They said he had eaten too many fried shrimp.

With as many people watching as possible, Billy stooped down and deposited some money in the trombone player's hat. Of course, he never let anybody, especially Sue Ellen, see what he put in there. He told her as he sat down "that was my last two-bits!" He lied often. What's the difference anyway, Sue Ellen was proud of him. Then he called for an order of two café lattes and one order of beignets with extra white stuff. The waiter scowled but lightened up when Billy gave him a dime under the table. He'd seen many rich folks do it and had watched how well it worked. It had the power to change some of the grumpiest faces in all the French Quarter into some of the happiest faces he had ever seen. He knew money made all the difference and at that age he wanted lots of it. But after he gave his heart to Jesus money really didn't matter all that much. It just helped him to live and buy food.

Years later he would see how unhappy Albright and Ernestine became even though they had more money than anyone in the whole State of Louisiana. And, besides, the Bible had told Billy not to "lay up treasures on earth." As he lay on his bed Billy suddenly realized the full impact of those words.

It was not that there was anything wrong with money. In fact he knew the Lord wanted many people to have lots of money. That's the way God blessed churches and charities like the rescue mission. Billy had been rescued many times and had no problem being very thankful. The older he got the more he realized God trusted some people with money. In many cases it seemed like the more God gave them the more they gave back to God through their churches and other places.

Like the one time when it seemed like days on end Billy had not one bite to eat. And then his Mama went out to all the garbage cans and found scraps of food. She called it "the scraps which fell from the rich man's table." Problem was his Mama had gotten so sick. It began with just a little nagging cough. Of course, when she became sick she couldn't stay home from work which was one problem. The other problem was they had no doctor or medicine or anything to help her. So she just got worse.

"Where's yer Mama?" Boudreaux asked because he had a real soft spot for Billy Bob's Mama. She always made him feel special and shared bits of their food with him even when it was only bits. Boudreaux didn't have a mother. In fact, Billy never heard him talk about his daddy either and so figured he didn't have a father, or, at least if he did he didn't act like he had one or maybe he was ashamed of him like he had done something awful or something. Billy's Mama told him the one thing you never do is ask about another boy's daddy. Never. Especially if the boy never said anything about having a daddy because that usually meant he either didn't have one or he was in prison or had done something real bad which was the reason why the boy would never mention him. Billy figured this was Boudreaux's situation and so he never asked him about his daddy.

And so with his Mama real sick here they were eating out of garbage cans. One day a kind man told them to go to the place where they give out hot soup and bread. Billy took it on himself to go and find it. It was called something like a kitchen and the day he went there was a whole line of what looked like rich people standing behind huge pots of the most delicious soup Billy had ever tasted. There were even some young people and kids serving as well. They all smiled when Billy came through the line and said nice things to make him feel real special. He asked if he could take some soup to his Mama because she was real sick. A kind lady said "most certainly, young man."

Then she put tin foil over a big bowl of the soup and added a few big chunks of bread. There was also a salad with real French dressing on it. It was the kind Billy really loved to eat because it had a sweet sort of taste that helped him get through salad stuff which was never his favorite food. He would never eat the stuff had his Mama not insisted because she said it was good for him. Billy and Boudreaux thought it was more like food for rabbits but ate it anyway because they were always so hungry.

Billy remembered how that kind lady had seen how sick his Mama was. She went and brought her car. It was a real fancy one with a radio. Billy had never driven in a car at that point and so the trip to the clinic made him think he was really somebody going overseas on an international journey in the lap of luxury. He decided not to tell Boudreaux because it would make him feel jealous or left out or that Billy and his Mama had suddenly gotten rich or something. That was part of their blood brother thing anyway that one would never make the other think he was into something rich which would leave the other one out. Blood brothers would never do that to each other.

So Billy grew up with a kind of affection for rich folks. This was the time his Mama was given all sorts of medicines and stuff with pills in it to make her better.

Twenty

As he lay on his bed the pain came in waves. By now his eyesight was just about gone. But not his memory. As he swallowed another tablet, Sue Ellen gently lifted his head so he could drink some water. He remembered how that lady had been so kind to his Mama.

"And I want you to know, young lady, not to worry about a thing. I have already instructed the medical staff to send all bills to me. It is my pleasure to take care of you and your boy. And, by the way, do drop by the kitchen on Thanksgiving Day. We are preparing a splendid meal!" With that she was gone and soon his Mama was well enough to move around again.

Billy never forgot that Thursday. He and his Mama went down to the kitchen at about eleven in the morning. What a feast they had with a whole bunch of the folks from the Quarter who had nowhere to eat. Billy's plate was loaded with turkey and dressing with gravy. There were green beans and carrots with piles of mashed potato. Not to mention the yams! Then they were served pumpkin pie in slices that looked like door stops. The lady was there and winked at Billy when she added a serious blob of vanilla bean ice cream on top of the pumpkin pie. Billy thought he was in another world. For the first time in living memory he and Boudreaux ate without saying one word. By the time he was through he was so stuffed he felt like he would burst like a popped balloon.

Once his Mama had found such happiness after going down front in the church it all began to make sense to Billy. Slowly. There were some real fine people in the world, he thought. And some of them were rich people.

From the time his Mama became a Christian she begged Billy to do the same. His life would never be worth much, she told him, without the Lord. It was just the way it was on the street. Some people were born with everything and some were not. Billy's mother had found peace even though she had nothing. She had become somebody, she said. Her greatest wish in life was for her Billy to have forgiveness and peace and know that one day he would go to heaven to live forever. She would try to teach her son about what the Bible says. Billy liked the part about the streets of heaven being paved with gold and stuff. Sometimes he would just sit on a bench in the park and imagine the pictures his mother had painted.

But he was stuck in a way of life. There was no way out. Born desperate and poor he would die desperate and poor. One small act of juvenile silliness led to another. Before long he and his friends became more daring.

Twenty One

It all came to a head during Mardi Gras. The whole city went wild during those two weeks and especially on Fat Tuesday. The preacher at his Mama's church said it was the time when the devil paid a personal visit to the Crescent City.

The thing about this Mardi Gras was the sickness of his mother. She had been to St. Luke's free medical clinic but the lump on her stomach had gotten bigger. The bleeding started the week before and Billy saw how the color had gone out of her face. The lump began to look like a football when his Mama told him she was going to meet Jesus. Billy Bob was beside himself and cried for the first time in many years. He also became really angry. Why, he asked? If there was a god where was he? His mother told him again about the Lord Jesus Christ. When Jesus died on the cross He had Billy Bob in mind. With a sweet smile on her face she motioned for her son to stand by her side and hold her hand. While he stood there she prayed for him and asked the Lord to save him so the two of them could spend all time and eternity in heaven together. She reminded Billy that she did not fear death because Jesus had given her eternal life. It was too much for the boy and he left the room walking head long into a troubled and ravenous city.

Millions of people had come from all over the world to dance and drink and go berserk. The Zulu parade was their favorite. While everyone crowded the streets and drank all day the boys did their work. It always proved very profitable as they picked pockets and stole everything one could imagine to their heart's content. But this was the Mardi Gras when all their luck would run out.

Billy's anger and frustration over his mother's illness may have driven him over the edge, but in later years Billy credited God with it all. They had watched the couple who stayed at the fancy hotel in the Quarter. Every night they went to parades and came back totally drunk. She would hang on his arm and they would be singing and rolling around the streets covered in beads and with pockets full of Mardi Gras doubloons. Sometimes they would make out right there in the street without any shame. So, long after midnight, the boys lay in wait and hit them hard. One good punch to the side of the face and the man went down without much of a fight. The woman laid a charge of rape against the boys but, even in his later years, Billy Bob vehemently denied the charge. Fortunately he was only charged as an accessory to the crime and so escaped the life sentence the two others received.

When the police picked Billy up he was hiding just off Willis road in a friend's shot-gun house. The judge showed no interest in what he had to say. Robbery and simple battery were serious and Billy walked out of the court room with a five year sentence. He began his term at the Juvenile prison in New Orleans.

Twenty Two

The only saving feature was the presence of Dwayne. Even in prison Billy's friend from down the Bayou was in charge. This was quickly established after one of the big eighteen year olds who thought he could challenge Dwayne ended up in the infirmary with multiple injuries to his face and legs. His one leg was so badly broken it looked like a match stick which had been snapped in two. The ragged, splintered edge of the bones protruded out where the muscle should have been while the foot, itself, had been ripped backwards and was touching the back side of his knee. They said he would never walk again. Of course no one could prove Dwayne had anything to do with it but every one knew it. So, Dwayne was a good ally to have on hand. Besides he really liked Billy Bob's style.

Just over one year into his time Billy was summoned into the warden's office. He had one set of handcuffs on his wrists with a set of chains wrapped around his waist. Then he had handcuffs placed on his ankles with a chain looped up to join the ones on his wrists. Billy felt like an animal. He was told when to get up and when to go to bed. He was told when to eat, what to eat, when to speak and how to dress. The place was filled with hostility and anger. Four letter words were the order of the day and fights were as frequent as the need to breathe. Standing there in the Warden's office with two officers at his side made Billy think hard and long about his life. But what he was about to hear took him over the edge. His Mama had died.

In the confines of his cell Billy broke down and wept for what seemed like hours on end. It seemed to him his whole life was a mess. He loved his mother so much. She had been everything to him. All he kept thinking about was how he had let her down. He could see her lying there with no one at her side. Her pain was extreme and Billy was not there to hold her hand. Then he remembered the blue colored tract she gave him. He took it out of the small toilet bag he was allowed to have in his cell.

It was folded neatly in four parts. Problem was he couldn't read it. But he could well recall the way his Mama would open it and read it to him. Not once but many times. He had heard her read it so many times you would think he was actually reading it himself. He would follow the lines from the bold, black ones to the small lines that weren't so big. It was the same question those seminary students had asked his mother so many years earlier. He also had listened to the preacher at his Mama's church on Elysian Fields Avenue on the east side of the city.

"How To Be Born Again" it said.

Sue Ellen shook him gently and told him to take his medicine. He tried to raise up on one arm but was too weak. Gently she put her left hand under his head and lifted it up so he could take a sip of whatever it was Mrs. Rhodes had left in the packet before the grieving family had left for the beach a few weeks before.

"I'm so glad Jesus came into my heart that day in prison", he whispered. She smiled lovingly at him and went back to the basin to get another warm cloth.

There were three things the tract his Mama had given him told him to do. First, he had to admit he was a sinner before God. Everybody was a sinner, according to the Bible. Then, he had to confess that sin to the Lord Jesus Christ. He remembered how many times his mother had spoken about the love of the Lord Jesus Christ who came to this earth as a baby. That's why Christmas had become so special to his mother. The reason Jesus came was so that He could die on a cross to forgive the sins of the world. One thing Billy understood was that Jesus was the only one in this world you could go to in order to receive total forgiveness of sins. That's why you had to confess your sins to Him. The third thing he had to do was to "trust Jesus by faith". This was the hardest because the preacher had said this meant you could do nothing except believe in your heart that Jesus was who He said He was. You also had to believe Jesus was alive and living in heaven where his Mama had just gone. When he hung around with some of the others and when he crept into the back of the church he heard them say you had to work and do stuff like give money if you wanted to know God. The tract said you didn't have to do anything except believe on Jesus. That was trust.

Billy sat in the corner of the cell next to the commode and cried until he could cry no more. The next day the officer came and said he could join with the others and go to the gym to hear a group of students who had traveled all the way from South Carolina to share some things with them in prison and sing.

The inmates came in rows with their hands behind their backs. Billy wore the green jumper because he was in for just one more year. The 'lifers' had to wear the red suits because they would be going on to Angola for a long time. The State pen in Louisiana was bad, they said. Rumor had it you went in and never came out. Simple as that! The boys were big there. And mean as snakes. And they loved it when the "babies" arrived fresh from the juvenile centers. Just the thought of going to Angola was enough to help some of them to reconsider doing anything foolish.

As he sat down on the floor he reached in his pocket to find the tract his Mama had given him. The one on "How To Be Born Again." That's when he realized he had left it next to the commode in the cell.

The chaplain took the stand and said how glad they were these young people had come to New Orleans. They went by the name of Mirror Image or something. Then he said to all the inmates and Billy and Dwayne they could be singing with Mirror Image "by the grace of God". Turning to the students he said, "ya'll could be one of these inmates were it not for the grace of God".

Billy remembered how that really got him thinking about his life and his Mama and God.

Then the group began to sing and dance. Some of the residents seated around Billy looked real bored to begin with and some looked mad. They began to laugh and jeer. Not even the officers seemed to care much. What really caught Billy's attention was when a pretty girl stood up and told them what a difference Jesus had made in her life especially after her own daddy had died. Another told them life without Jesus was worthless. They sang some great songs they all knew. One boy even played the sax just like they did in the quarter and Billy Bob thought how much money this boy could make if he played outside Café Du Monde. Mirror Image kind of talked in a way everybody could understand. Then they sang a song which asked a question. It had to do with whether or not Billy would be prepared to hand his life over to Jesus.

"Will you be the one?" was the question the song asked.

Then the preacher of the group stood up. He talked real straight and direct. Everybody listened. The preacher spoke about respecting others. He said Jesus had given him respect for all people. It didn't matter where they came from or how much money they had or what color they were. Billy realized just how much he had hated certain types of people.

Then he spoke about love. He said the greatest love of all was when the Lord Jesus gave His life for all people. Billy thought of his mother. Then the preacher laid down the smack on all the inmates. That was when he began to talk about hope. He made sense to Billy when he pointed out just how hopeless most people were. Lots of people were searching for something and wanted to have meaning in life. That got Billy's attention. But when he went on about the absolute certainty of life after death Billy sat up real good. He realized his mother was with the Lord Jesus. He wanted to see her again. The preacher made the point real strong that when you give your heart to Jesus it meant you not only go to heaven yourself, but you get to spend "all time and eternity" with those you love that may have already died. That was all he needed to hear.

When they all bowed their heads the preacher asked if there was anyone who would give his heart and life to Jesus. All of a sudden Billy felt overcome with a sense of his own sin. He knew he didn't stand a chance by himself. Jesus loved him and died for him. That was it. He heard himself repeating the prayer with the preacher.

"Dear God: I know I am a sinner. I've messed up. Everybody has messed up. I'm tired of running. I'm tired of being lonely. I know you died on a cross just for someone like me. I believe you love me. I believe God raised Jesus from the dead. Please come into my heart and save me right now. I put my trust in you. I pray these things in Jesus name. Amen."

In that same moment Billy Bob was saved. He knew it in his heart.

Many years later Billy found himself thinking about his time in prison. It never stopped amazing him just how he came to give his heart to Jesus. As he lay on his death-bed he turned to his wife and smiled again.

"You need anything, Sugar Lump?" she asked.

"Not a thing, Sweetness," he replied. But the pain got the better of him and for the first time he coughed uncontrollably. "It's just that I'm so glad I gave my heart and life to Jesus way back then," he exclaimed in between each cough. He smiled again.

"Now what's going on in that head of yours?" Sue Ellen queried with a glint in her eye.

"Oh, I was just thinking about how Dwayne got saved that day too."

Billy remembered how restless Dwayne was during the presentation by Mirror Image. He hated all that religious stuff. Little did he know God was at work. Half way through the program Dwayne persuaded the guard to let him go to the toilet. Permission granted, he was forced to use the only one available. Yup! The one Billy Bob had come from. The one where he had left the tract his mother gave him on "How To Be Born Again." Billy could never get over how Dwayne had given his heart and life to Jesus right there in the juvenile prison. He was a changed man.

The last year the two of them were inside they led many inmates to know Jesus. For years Billy heard about Dwayne even though their paths would seldom cross. Billy was too poor to go anywhere. Evidently Dwayne met a beautiful Christian girl by the name of Sylvia. She was a preacher's daughter. Dwayne went on to the seminary in New Orleans and became the first member of his family to get so much education. Last Billy heard he was a pastor with many children and a great preacher. Many people had come to know Jesus because of the testimony of Dwayne. Billy knew he would be reunited in heaven with his friend. Probably really soon.

Twenty Three

The first thing he saw when he walked out of prison was Sue Ellen. It was like she had been waiting for him. He asked her to marry him. She said, "Yes!"

They were so poor they sneaked into the cathedral late one night and performed their own wedding ceremony. Sue Ellen put on her favorite dress. The one with the pink flowers on it. She even had a red bow to put in her hair. Billy rolled up some old copper wire to make a ring and bought one flower from the man on the corner.

Sue Ellen's Mama came with them to be a witness and gave the couple ten dollars she had saved up for a wedding present. She also invited them to honeymoon in her little room stuck away in the back streets of the French Quarter. Their wedding "feast" comprised a hot dog from the vendor who had built quite a reputation selling the "best dad gum dogs east of the Mississippi." His "claim to fame" was the number of times Senator Long had made a special trip just for the purpose of devouring at least three of his 'dogs'. The relish was ranked in the top echelon of bayou 'dogs,' according to informed sources.

The couple was stuck in a never ending cycle of the most wretched poverty. No education, no money, no car to drive, no work, no family except Sue Ellen's sickly Mama, and no hope, if the truth were to be made known. But they had each other. Above all, the two of them had a deep and abiding love for the Lord Jesus Christ. In his quiet way, Billy Bob went about his daily search for employment. A little bit of this. A little bit of that.

Twenty Four

Billy Bob was a changed man, that was one thing for certain. His all time favorite thing to do was to tell people about his best friend. Most figured it was Boudreaux or Dwayne (whom he hadn't seen in years) or maybe even his wife. Sue Ellen was highly regarded by the folks out on the street because she was different. Always had a smile on her face, they all said, even though she was one of them and poor and all. But, no sir, his best friend wasn't any of those people. Billy loved to keep them guessing.

"Ya'lls wanna know whose is fer sure mah bes friend," he would inquire with a twinkle in his eye.

"Shoot, Billy'" would often be the come back, "Man like you got lotsa friends. You being so kind and caring and all that."

Hardly a person out there hadn't noticed the change in Billy since he had gotten out of prison. "Went in bad and came out good," was the word in the Quarter.

Billy loved to talk to the preacher at his church on Elysian Fields Avenue. All he wanted to do was tell all the folks about the Lord. But with his lack of education and training he figured it was impossible. Besides he couldn't even read and write. So what good could he do?

One day the preacher invited both him and Sue Ellen to come to the church every Monday night for thirteen weeks to be trained in how to talk to people about the Lord. Some of the seminary people were going to teach them, he said. That suited

Billy because he would never forget what they had done that day when they talked to his Mama out there in the middle of the French Quarter. He could never get over the fact those young men bothered with people like him and his Mama. He had almost become used to the way rich folks would look them up and down for the most part. Some of them would look the other way or just pretend to be looking at something else or nothing, for that matter.

He couldn't blame them really. Most people like Billy looked bad. Real bad, some of them. And they all had their stories about sick Mamas in Ohio or some place nobody had ever heard of, and they hadn't seen in a long time, and if they couldn't get a bus ticket their Mama would die. The yarns about children always worked magic in the Quarter because most had kids.

Besides there were best and worst times to launch an offensive in an effort to scrounge a few dollars here and there. Like when these folks stepped out of one of the top restaurants like Ralph and Kacoos or Masperos or Landrys or one of them. The Chart House right on the corner next to the Cathedral was a great spot because there was always some little fellow tap dancing and offering to tell them "were they got them shoes." So money was usually forthcoming when those folks were "ripe and ready fer da pickin' " Boudreaux surmised.

"When dey come outta dat place der wit dem toofpicks pickin out da crawdads from der teef an stuff, ya gotta hit 'em man cause dats wen dey ripe fer da pickin jus like dem strewberries dat com ripe fer da pickin up der in Ponchatoula. Yeh man, de's be somtin real good too when des ripe. I do garontee dis man. When dat belly's full wit dem crawdads an frog legs da greenbacks done get to flow down to mah pocket. I like dat!"

"Jus catch 'em wit der pants down," he regularly announced as the team readied themselves for another day of free-will offerings.

"Watch for a loaded belly, a loaded mind and a loaded wallet," became the coded watchword on the street.

It wasn't difficult to put all three ingredients together. There was plenty of good food, plenty of half naked females around every corner designed to load even the most chaste minds with lustful thoughts, and plenty of money being thrown around like it grew on trees. It always amazed Billy how everyone always seemed to complain about the economy and the price of gas and the lousy job the president and governor were doing, but they always seemed to have no problem spending all sorts of money on a bunch of junk at the best of times.

Men were particularly bad when in those joints and things like where his Mama had to take off all her clothes when he was a kid. He'd watch as the men would whoop and holler and throw money at his Mama and the others.

But Billy's life had changed completely. And when it did he suddenly found himself wanting to learn more about Jesus. He especially wanted to know how to tell others about how to give their hearts and lives to Jesus. So when the preacher told him and Sue it was those seminary boys who would teach him he needed to hear no more. Besides he often wished he could be like them some day.

They called it with letters. They were CWT which he soon learned stood for Continuous Witness Training. This presented Billy with his first big problem because he had to go over that a hundred times just to learn how to say it all fancy. Problem was all the others were writing and had pens and books to read. All Billy had was a good set of ears and a wife who thought he was the best thing since the invention of peanut butter. And when one of them came in new and didn't know Billy couldn't read or write his sweet wife would just jump in and answer for him.

Sue Ellen taught him to learn what CWT stood for by saying "Call William Today." That was easy for Billy because his real name was William, as in William Terence Malkmus. He felt real educated when he remembered what CWT stood for.

They even had to learn verses in the Bible which made Billy really happy. All he really cared about was telling people about Jesus.

The day finally came when some of the folks went out to visit some people and tell them about Jesus using all they had learned in CWT. When they walked up to the door of the first house the others were all afraid but not Billy. He was a lot of things but one thing he was not. He was not scared of anybody. Especially seeing he was so excited about telling them about Jesus.

A big man opened the door and glared at the group of three people. Billy was so excited he announced they were there to "Call William Today." Then he fumbled around and said he had made a mistake. The man was not happy. So Billy just looked at him and said all he knew to say.

"Would you like to give your heart to Jesus, Sir?" Billy inquired in his broken Cajun English.

The man looked around like he all of a sudden had been hit on the head with a sledge hammer. He began to stammer. Then he asked Billy how he knew about him. Billy said he didn't but wanted to tell the man about how to give his heart to Jesus.

Right there it happened. On his doorstep on Franklin Avenue. The man bowed his head and asked Jesus to save him from his sin. The next Sunday he came to church with his wife and never stopped coming after that event.

So that's how Billy came to asking people about whether they knew who his best friend was.

"Wanna know who's my best friend?" he would ask of scores and scores of people

Then came the break they had been waiting for. It began with a simple phone call. The voice reported the need for a live-in maid. The master of the house was a young business man who lived with his bride. Their home was situated just off St. Charles Avenue in the beautiful Garden District in New Orleans.

Thus began the intertwined saga of two men. One became very rich. The other remained very poor. They both died.

PART TWO

THE RICH MAN DIED AND WAS BURIED. THE
POOR MAN DIED AND WAS CARRIED BY THE
ANGELS INTO THE PLACE WHERE GOD IS.

One

A trip to Monaco was commonplace to Albright A. Rhodes.
He had flown there so many times and had grown to really love the place for many reasons. Money certainly was not
the least of his problems. His investments had paid off handsomely. But this particular trip would change his life forever.

Unfortunately Ernestine's passion for shopping and her
unbridled compulsion to outdo the Cartwright family meant
the stop in London or Paris was obligatory. She and her entourage could be seen visiting one department store after the
other just off Regents Street in London. Harrods was her favorite, not so much because of the goods available but because
of the prestige it afforded her when she went back to New Orleans and was able to report the details of her adventures to her
tea-party friends.

The day in London was never complete without afternoon tea at the Ritz which included scones, strawberry jam and the best of Scotland's clotted cream. She loved the feeling afforded by the hotel's opulence and was often heard offering a little squeak of pleasure when the ladies-in-waiting brought forth the tea in magnificent rose-colored china. As far as the sandwiches were concerned nothing could top the smoked salmon. It was brought in from the mountainous lochs perched way above her favorite Scottish get-away.

The Kinnaird Estate was an elegant family home, built in 1770 near the River Tay, just three miles outside Dunkeld, in beautiful Perthshire. It offered majestic views of the Scottish Highlands while set in the midst of its own 9000 acre estate. Albright loved the loch fishing, deer stalking and lovely country walks.

Paris was another story. After her regular stop at the Louvre she would stroll in and out of some of the more prestigious shops on the Champs Elysees. The wife of Mister Albright A. Rhodes was always accompanied by an entourage of aides who were handed package after package. She would have considered anything less uncivilized. They trailed after her like a gaggle of obedient young geese following their mother in humble adoration and dutiful expectation. The black limousine slowly followed the shopping party, ready at a moment's notice to receive its treasured cargo of new outfits, an assortment of jewelry, and every kind of French perfume known to women.

Together with a few hand selected friends she would dine at Les Ambassadeurs just off the corner of the rue Boissy-d'Anglas and the place de la Concorde. The elegance afforded by this former ballroom of the eighteenth century had so many culinary creations, Ernestine could hardly contain herself. She particularly loved the "la charlotte de crabe et tomate, cremeaux au jus de carapaces", or the "le millefeuille au chocolat Manjari, compote de pommes cuites a la facon Tatin." And the wines were out of this world, she would say.

It was not uncommon for Albright to pay a courtesy call on the Prime Minister when in London. Harold Wilson had been particularly enamored with Rhodes, especially during the

Rhodesian crisis in the sixties. During the negotiations with Ian Smith prior to his unilateral declaration of independence, Albright A. Rhodes was often seen alongside the Prime Minister. Besides they shared a love for the deep flavored Rhodesian pipe tobacco with its rich aromatic taste.

Secretly, Mister Rhodes was an admirer of Smith. He loved his tenacity and the daring with which he confronted the Patriotic Front led by Robert Mugabe and Joshua Nkomo. It always seemed ironic that Nkomo fled into exile in England after Mugabe took over the new country of Zimbabwe.

On one trip to Salisbury, the capital of Southern Rhodesia, Albright had flown on a military helicopter to the Victoria Falls region and had met personally with the commander of the crack Selous Scouts. Lieutenant Colonel Mike Statton had become a legend in his own time. His disciplined troops were ready for action at a moment's notice. They were tough, well trained in bush warfare and continually on the move.

But when Albright was with Wilson he pandered to his British indignation at the shocking and outrageous manner with which the Smith government had seized control and declared itself independent from the motherland. One thing Albright understood was the meaning of "playing his cards" at the right time in the right place. His motto encompassed the idea of taking care of number one whatever the cost.

He would often tell his sons, "Never forget who you are! You're a Rhodes. When all is said and done you owe nothing to anybody. When they fall like flies around you make certain you are the one left standing up tall and straight! Money is what it is all about. Make as much of it as you can and don't let anyone try to tell you what to do with it or where to spend it. Above all, watch out for the leaches! They are the lazy no good bums who refused to work and sacrifice. Don't let the poor and wretched distract you. Don't get me wrong boys! Help people when you can but keep control. You will always have the poor with you. So, hold on to what you've got. Just look at me, boys! Just look at your Daddy!"

Albright retained a special relationship with most of the British prime ministers from both the Whigs and the Tories. Callaghan did not quite see eye to eye with him but he deeply admired the iron lady, Margaret Thatcher and her successor, John Major. He particularly loved it when Major would invite him to accompany him while he enjoyed his favorite past time. They would sit in the box at the world renowned Lord's Cricket ground and chat for hours while cheering on the English Eleven. Cricket seemed so civilized to Albright. He had great admiration for the way in which the outfielders would catch that hard cricket ball coming at them at full pace, with their bare hands. He and the Prime Minister would trade jokes and make all kinds of comments about the merits and differences between English cricket and America's favorite pasttime.

"Need to teach those chaps over there to play a real gentlemen's sport!" Major would blurt out between puffs on his pipe.

"No time available!" counteracted Albright. "Our boys believe in work. That's why America has so much, John. Now you know why we sent our boys over to bail you out when Churchill came crying. If we played cricket we wouldn't have had time to train our troops and build the arms to rescue you. You were so busy playing cricket and drinking tea you forgot there's a world out there!"

Not to be outdone by his rich American friend Major's calculating mind went into high gear.

"Your lads are a bunch of sissies. Need to teach your chaps to catch those fly balls without having a bucket tied to their hands. Real men do it bare handed. Besides, old chap, just think how much more exciting baseball would be if at the bottom of the ninth, bases loaded, two outs and trailing by three runs the batter hits a colossal fly ball. Take the bucket away and the question becomes anything but a foregone conclusion. Will he hold on to the ball?"

And so it went on.

Their favorite country, somehow, was still Italy. Especially the coastline between Saint Tropez and Monaco. The French Riviera suited him just fine. "Something about the feel of it," he would often remark. Many times they would follow the coast towards Beaulieu after landing at the Nice Cote d'Azur airport just eight miles away. The elegance, refinement and gentle way of life captured by the decor of the beautiful Florentine La Reserve de Beaulieu suited Ernestine especially. On other occasions they would spend a month or so at the former residence of the Templar Knights. The La Chateau du Domaine St. Martin provided them with a suite that had a panoramic view across some eighty miles of Italian hills and coastline. The wines weren't all that bad either.

Albright loved to be included in the lives of the rich and famous and, while he would certainly never admit to it, he had an uncanny knack of being in the right place at the right time. The picture of him kissing the hand of Raquel Welch at the Cannes Film festival and the one of him dancing with Brigitte Bardot even made its way into Time Magazine, much to his hidden delight.

One day he struck gold.

The owner of Texas Mete bought the magnificent Miramare Hotel in San Remo. It stood proudly on the lower slopes of the mountain range that seemed to run all along that part of the Mediterranean seacoast. From every angle, particularly from the sea, the long white columns strutted their magnificence like a proud peacock trying to impress his harem. Spectacular views of the Mediterranean provided him with a logical place to send the type of customers whose potential was worth a little "wining and dining." The railroad that ran past the front gate of the hotel between the lower gardens and the private beach provided a natural convenience for the company to "ship" in any and all supplies to suit any and all individual tastes and needs. Unknown to his wife this would even include the appropriate Italian girls who could arrive and depart on the train without much outside attention. Albright's senior associate would set the whole affair in order so the customer would be catered to and pampered to the hilt.

This trip was different, however. Albright A. Rhodes was a dying man.

Rhodes was a fiercely proud but private man. Even though his inheritance had been no small matter, many believed his marriage into the Rothschild family was little more than good luck. To him, this was no accident. And his enormous wealth was certainly not simply because of his wife's inheritance. Some people just have a lot more luck than others. He repeatedly told this to his kids. Their mother's father had indeed bequeathed his entire fortune to his son-in-law, but it was a minuscule amount compared to what it had become. He'd moved the outfit to New Orleans after all. Here he was in his seventies and most of the world knew about him. Thousands clamored for his attention and requests for money blew across his desk like packs of hyenas in a frenzied search for a bone.

Two

Albright tried to sit up. From the balcony of the Miramare he could see some of the exquisite yachts sailing by on their way to the warmer waters off Sicily. His private suite on the top floor, in addition to having six large bedrooms with every convenience, had a wrap around balcony which accentuated the view of the Mediterranean.

To his right the water way led these floating multi-million dollar condominiums to the pampered docks that bordered Prince Rainier's small kingdom of Monte Carlo To his immediate front lay rows of beautiful topless women soaking up the sun without one thought of its rays deadly consequences. Their men played volley ball and jostled for attention while flexing every muscle in their well oiled bodies. The rocks which jutted out in various irregular patterns into the deep blue sea looked like unwelcome guests at a formal dinner party. And yet, strangely, the longer one gazed upon them the more they seemed to fit.

His whole body ached. He was a sick man. He knew it. But he had been too proud to admit he wasn't well. Besides, time was on his side. And, he would convince himself, some of his closest friends were the most famous physicians in the world. Besides, he was busy. Very busy. Albright didn't pay too much attention to his health.

It was not that he was over weight. Tennis kept him reasonably fit and sturdy. He ate well. Very well, in fact. His diet was relatively low in carbohydrates and fats. He seldom had the need to eat fast foods and never indulged in excessive amounts of fried foods and junk food. His culinary tastes always presented him with delicious little delicacies in small, but regular amounts. Besides all this, he had his personal trainer, John, who owned and operated the Nautilus Fitness Center on the corner of Washington and Tchouptoulas in the Garden District. John had to have been the most compassionate and caring man Albright had ever met in his entire life. His personal dietician, Marilyn, was equally caring and very dedicated to her work. And so between John and Marilyn, Rhodes considered himself in good hands.

But in spite of all his personal pampering, his health began to deteriorate rapidly while he was still in Europe. One day, while sitting in the living room of the Miremare, he knew something was really wrong with his body. It was deep down. He was losing weight fairly rapidly, felt very weak and just couldn't seem to get up in the mornings. Fatigue was foreign to him. Perhaps what worried him most of all was the continual pain in his lower back, and, even, on occasion, all the way down his leg. It was like it was in his spinal column. Tylenol became ineffective. Albright acknowledged at last that something would have to be done.

Twenty hours later, his plane touched down at the New Orleans International Airport.

Three

Doctors Harry K. Taylor and William S. Huey were not only two of Rhodes' closest friends, but were also considered to be amongst the most gifted physicians in America. They had traveled the world together and loved to play golf at English Turn. The only thing that separated them was the doctors' unapologetic faith and trust in God. Their commitment to their church in service and financial giving was something of an amusement to Albright. To be fair, though, there were many times when the business community of their church had been called on to rally around special projects and such. Albright always led the way especially when approached by his pastor or these close friends of his. From time to time Taylor and Huey would challenge Rhodes concerning his faith. But Albright was a master at giving the right answer designed to placate them or "get them off his back" as he put it to others. As far as he was concerned there was nothing worse than someone who "went overboard" with their Christianity. But it never interfered with their friendship.

So when Albright called on them their attention was immediate. Their office was just down the road from the estate on the corner of Camp and Magazine. When he entered Taylor's office through the private side door it bothered him to have to admit he wasn't doing too well.

"Hey Al," quipped Harry. "How's the pizza in Italy these days?"

"Not bad, not bad," came the reply.

"Come on now Al! You look like you seen a ghost, man. Need to talk, huh?"

"Yup, sure do, Harry. But I don't quite know what to say. Just feel awful Harry!"

Harry's trained eye could see beyond the spoken word. It had been four months since Rhodes had set off for England and Italy. And the month prior to that Harry and William had taken their wives to Bermuda for a two week vacation. They stayed at Cambridge Beach, in Somerset County and had an incredible time snorkeling, jet skiing, riding scooters around the island and getting thoroughly trounced at croquet by a South African born expert.

"How much weight have you lost?" the doctor inquired.

"I guess about twenty five or so. Haven't weighed in lately Harry. But none of my clothes fit me real well. Just feel so weak. And have this kind of stabbing pain in my back and leg. Hard to put my finger on it though. But the pain is pretty bad. Made me fly home at once. Just had to see you Harry. You know money isn't an issue. Just call a spade a spade Harry. Tell me what's up. I can take it. You know me well enough and I trust you Harry. But listen, Harry. Confidential is the name of the game. It's my reputation, you know. And the business. Stocks and all that. They get word I'm down and down they go. You know what I'm saying Harry? Not even the wife. No Sir! Just the two of us, O.K.?"

Harry looked grave. His friend needed help, that much he knew. But if his hunch was correct nothing else would really matter any more.

"Look, Al, let's get started then. I'm going to need to examine you and I want to begin by checking your prostate. We have to do this Al. It's pretty straight forward. You've had this before even though a long time ago. I checked your charts. It was about seven years ago Al. Your PSA was up if you remember. You have any problems when you go to the bathroom, Al?"

"Guess I do, Harry. Just don't seem to be able to empty my bladder."

"Well let's just go back seven years Al. According to my records I put you on Depo Lupron. Remember that?"

"Remind me about that one Harry. What exactly did it do for me? Seemed to work, whatever it is."

Albright kind of perked up a bit. Last time he took those shots his problems seemed to go away.

"Like that," he thought. "Suits me."

Harry sat on the edge of his desk. He had a white doctor's coat on with the name Harry K. Taylor emblazoned on the left side and "Urology" clearly spelled out underneath his name. In his hand he held a vanilla folder with the name Albright A. Rhodes written in blue ink.

"The Depo Lupron we gave you was essentially designed to stop the pituitary stimulation of the testicles, Al. Remember that's where some 97% of all testosterone in your body is produced. This is what feeds the prostate, much like gasoline runs an engine. Each time we gave you a shot of this Depo Lupron medication it blocked the pituitary testicular axis and effectively stopped the production of the testosterone thus removing the hormonal stimulation of the cancer. As such, Al, it had a dramatic effect in reducing the cancer itself. We always hope this will contain the cancer, but, sometimes it can come back. What we don't want to happen is for the cancer to get outside the prostate. Once it does it can get into the lymphatic system and ultimately into the bones, which means it's off and running."

"You think mine is off and running, Harry?" Albright asked. He moved a little in his chair and Harry thought he detected a hint of fear in his voice. Not that he didn't understand the concern on Albright's part. If the cancer had come back and was, indeed, outside the prostate, this would not be a pleasant thing to have to tell his friend.

Harry realized every patient was different in the way they responded. He'd tried to level with Rhodes seven years earlier. But trying to impress him with the seriousness with his adeno carcinoma was harder than trying to get a five hundred pound hog to march down an executioner's runway in order to be shot in the head and provide some Englishman with a good plate of bacon for breakfast. He had lost count of the numbers of times he had insisted Albright come and see him for a check up. At this point, his gut feeling was not good.

In the privacy of his office Albright submitted to his expertise. The discomfort he experienced when contact was made with his prostate was as severe as he had ever known.

"I'm sending you for a bone scan, Al," Harry said after telling Rhodes he thought the matter warranted serious and immediate attention.

"We need to diagnose your situation more definitively."

"Is this like an X-ray?" inquired the now somber business man.

"No, Al. It's a nuclear medicine scan which images the given area. The patient is given some intravenous mildly radioactive material that will tag the prostate cancer cells. If the bone scan is positive, the bones will actually show a dark area. In other words it "lights up" the problem, so to speak. The affected areas are shown up."

All of a sudden Albright wanted to call his pastor. He hadn't been to church in about a year and had not even seen the pastor in months but he'd been busy. Everybody knew that. Besides he had been overseas. But, there again, maybe he was overreacting.

When the report came back it was even worse than Harry had thought it would be.

Rhodes' love affair with his own sense of immortality had been rudely interrupted. All of a sudden he no longer wanted to be going all the time. Trips out of town were unthinkable. He had been forced to tell Ernestine the basics, but only on condition she say nothing to the family. He mooched around the house going from study to bathroom to sunroom to boardroom to bathroom to game room and back to bathroom. At night he was more up than down. He constantly felt like he needed to urinate but could not seem to empty his bladder. He developed more headaches and back aches but would not discuss the matter with his wife. At times he would become angry and hostile. He began to say mean things to her and even accused her of wishing him dead.

"I know exactly what you're going to do the moment I pop off. Marry that stinking Cajun! And don't try to deny it. Well let me tell you something, woman. Not you, or anyone is going to have my money. It's mine. Always has been. Don't think I'm stupid! Think your Daddy was this and that! If it wasn't for me you'd end up like that sorry maid of yours. That's right. That wretched little stinky maid who was born in a garbage can in the French Quarter. Not to mention that holier-than-thou live in of hers!"

"Billy Bob is not her live in. They are married in the eyes of God, Albright."

"There you go bringing up God again. Think I'm stupid, huh? Soon as you lose you bring up the big man in the sky. I'm sick of it. Leave me alone! And for that matter tell God to leave me alone. And if that sorry son of a sea-faring catfish, that low down lazy Billy Bob ever so much as mentions the name of God to me again, so help me I'll have his guts for garters!"

A loud knock at the door interrupted the tirade. He yelled at Sue Ellen to see who it was.

Four

In stepped the Reverend Benjamin D. Franks, pastor of their church. "Just heard through the grapevine about your situation, Albright. Came by to tell you how glad I am to have you back in town. Was just out and about and thought I'd pop in and see how you and Ernestine are doing. Perhaps we could have a word of prayer together."

Albright squirmed. He felt anger rising in his stomach. It was one thing to be visited by the pastor, another thing to be exposed in front of his wife, and, entirely another to be forced to submit to prayer. One thing his wife knew was that neither of them gave much credence to prayer. She was just more genteel when it came to spiritual matters.

"Well preacher," Albright announced, "you know I believe in God. Wouldn't be a deacon if I wasn't, would I? Appreciate you coming by. Doc says my problem is not uncommon. Sure to mend pretty soon. Appreciate you having a little chat with the big man upstairs. You have a direct line to him, I know. It all helps. And, by the way, you know that mission thing you talked about. That group of kids going with the team to build that church in Montana. Me and the wife would like to underwrite all the expenses and also pay for the construction which, I believe, is somewhere around fifty thousand?"

He called for Peter, his personal accountant. Peter came in from the library and was immediately instructed to write a check in the amount of seventy-five thousand dollars to the church.

"Thanks so much, Albright. You and Ernestine are such a blessing." And they were, indeed. Their pastor had never questioned the motive with which they gave of their financial resources. He knew the Lord had raised up some folks with a special gift, not only to make much money, but to give it away. The Rhodes' were a generous couple. Thousands of charities had benefited, as had the church. Their money was honestly gained, at least to the knowledge of the pastor. Uncle Sam had never questioned their integrity.

What bothered Benjamin Franks was the issue of Albright's spiritual standing. Of course he believed God was the only one who would really know. But Rhodes seldom showed any real spiritual interest. He had no apparent desire to see others come to know the Lord Jesus. He never witnessed to others and he and Ernestine never opened their home for spiritual functions, like discipleship groups and such. Social gatherings and youth related functions like sleepovers for the girls and swim parties were always welcome.

Following the prayer the pastor retired to his car. As he drove down the tree lined driveway a deep sense of sadness filled his heart. He hated to see a man like Albright suffer so much. But it was more than just the suffering. The clergyman grieved for the business man's soul.

Five

His condition began to deteriorate. The family became concerned. Trips to the doctor were more frequent. The cancer had spread.

Gradually Albright became more and more anemic. The cancer was replacing the bone marrow. As a result it was taking over the hemoglobin producing marrow cells. He became constantly fatigued and had no energy to do things he had been accustomed to doing all his life.

One morning his leg broke. Just like that. He simply stepped out of bed and it snapped. The cancer had literally eaten the bone away.

The pathological fracture he suffered caused him to scream in pain. He became more and more miserable. The pain was extreme. It became so bad that Harry admitted him into Oschner Hospital. His private room was more like a suite and had a magnificent view overlooking the mighty Mississippi River. At least the grand kids could stand in front of the big window and watch all the oil tankers and barges chugging up the river towards Baton Rouge or down towards the port of New Orleans and ultimately the Gulf of Mexico.

The hospital staff tried to medicate him as best they could. The oral medications he had been given while at home provided some relief but now Harry wanted to administer spot radiation or palliative radiation directed at the specific areas revealed by the bone scan.

The medical personnel knew this would only be a temporary stop gap measure designed to make their patient feel better. His condition was serious. He was a dying man.

As soon as Rhodes made it back home he wheeled himself outside to the rose garden. He loved both the tranquility and the fragrance generated by his favorite flowers. It had been a long and difficult stay at Oschner, so this little respite was, indeed, most welcome.

The morning sun was glorious. A gentle breeze caressed the tips of the trees like the gentle stroke of a mother's hand as she tended her distraught child. The pink, orange, white and red rose petals appeared to respond in kind to their honored guest. They emitted their perfume in silent wafts of aromatic splendor causing the whole lower garden to erupt in nature's glory. In humble obedience to the one who had made it possible for them to display their fragrant magnificence, rows upon rows of them seemed to bow their heads as they curtsied before their king like beautiful ladies in the Palace of Versailles prostrating themselves before Louis XIV.

Albright's peace and solitude was suddenly shattered. Whistling. Not now, dadgumit, he thought. Not now!

"Howya doin' Mister Albright, Sah?"

Rhodes spun around in his chair. Surely not, he thought as anger began to well up inside him. Leave me in peace, his heart cried out. The last thing he needed was a conversation with Billy Bob. And quit whistling that infernal "amazing grace" song.

"Dadgumit," he thought.

But what he saw shocked him. His long time gardener was a shell of a man. Albright figured he'd lost at least one hundred pounds. Nothing but skin and bone. And his skeleton was wedged between two sticks that had been constructed into some kind of make shift pair of crutches. Further observation revealed a missing leg just below the knee cap and various other notable infectious looking things too ghastly to comprehend.

"Don't look too good yourself, Billy," he replied with a look on his face that resembled a cross between bulldog's expression and the face of a seventy nine year old man who had just taken a bite out of an extremely sour lemon. Just listening to the old man talk with that "cajun-French Quarter-cross between jam-balaya and picante source kind of accent" was enough aggravation for a culture vulture such as himself.

"Ah nah Sah, I been jus fine though I tenk ya fer ya kindness. Now, Sah, Mister Albright, my sweet little wife's been tellin me yalls not doin so fine Mister Albright. Dis why wen I sees ya out here just sniffin up dem sweetness dat dem rosies let loos off I jus come a runnin caus I bes prayin fer ya ever day. And nites too I must add. An dat goes fer da wife too now Mister Albright."

"Dadgumit, you idiot!" he almost swore but then checked himself. The one thing he would never do is lower himself into the same pig-pen he believed the old man had been born in.

"Well I'm not just fine. I'm dying man. Doctor says the cancer has done its work. I'm so dad gum mad. But I thank you for asking. You can go now Billy. And don't lie to me! Don't tell me you are fine when it doesn't take a rocket scientist to figure out you got problems too."

"Ah nah, Sah. I's jus fine," Billy Bob replied with a pleasant smile on his old cracked face.

Albright was not far off the mark, though. One look at Billy left no room for speculation. His landlord might have spent half his life cultivating a disdain for the poor man but, even he knew something had changed. His gardener had always been sprightly, to say the least. From the day he first arrived on the estate Rhodes had never heard even so much as a veiled complaint. Or even an opinion disguised as a hint. About anything. He had to give him that much. And what with minimum wage and little else to show for it, even Albright had to have just a little admiration tucked away somewhere. The only reason he had felt compelled to keep him was because he was useful, and reliable. And he had green fingers and all that.

Of course there was also the real reason. Sue Ellen. But that was no one else's business and he had succeeded in keeping it that way. It was the least he could do to honor his father's memory. That business trip to New Orleans so many years ago. The promise he made to his daddy just moments before he died

He looked at Billy Bob again. On the outside his polished and fine tuned cultural heritage presented a look of accommodation and resignation. To tell him to get lost would be unbecoming a man of his stature. Besides he had long gone settled the issue. Termination would have been too risky. The payout was worth the trouble of having to listen to that infernal whistling of those "dadgum hymns" all the time.

And then there was Ernestine. Their marriage had its fair share of ups and downs. But they had stuck it out at least. The children were paramount anyway. What went on behind closed doors, even he admitted, was rather cosmetic. But what the heck, he would assure himself. He'd had other ways and means to have fun. Especially in Italy.

The pain was back. Excruciating pain. His peace and quiet gone.

"Let me ask you something, Billy," the one dying man asked of the other dying man.

"Yah Sah, Mister Albright. Ya know I's always bes vailible wen yas comes a callin."

"How come you can smile like that when the whole world can see you're a sick man, huh?"

"It's all about my best friend, Mister Albright."

"And who might that be?" inquired the chief executive officer and owner of Texas Mete.

"Well his name is Jesus, Sir. You see many years ago he came into my heart and gave me more peace and joy than I could ever stand. He changed my life completely."

Fat lot of good that did him, thought Albright. Just one look at him was enough. Pathetic. Spent his entire life groveling and scrounging for a morsel. If it weren't for the crumbs which fell from Albright's table, so to speak, this man would have less than nothing.

Friend? What friend? This explained why Albright had never felt good about going overboard with religion. Nothing worse than a maniac about religion, was his often spoken opinion. He could never stand those fundamentalists who stuck

their noses into everything where they shouldn't be. Just thinking about it made him mad.

Billy Bob went on to explain how he had been told about
the disease he had. His diabetes was killing him. He knew he
was about to die.

"I know that, Mister Albright. Yup, I'm an old man but God
has given me a good life. And a wonderful wife in Sue Ellen.
She's been next to me all the way through. We pray every day
and thank the Lord Jesus for all he has done for us. We are just
so blessed in every way. Wouldn't have it any other way. You
know one of my favorite hymns goes like this.

"What a friend we have in Jesus
All our sins and griefs to bear;
What a privilege to carry
Everything to God in prayer
O' what peace we often forfeit
O' what needless pain we bear
All because we do not carry
Everything to God in prayer.

"You see, Mister Albright, Sir, this is why I have a smile
on my face. Because Jesus died on the cross for me and because I have trusted him as my personal Lord and Savior, I
am forgiven forever. Now what that means is that when I die,
which is coming up real soon, I am going to heaven to be
with Jesus forever. I have nothing to fear. I have nothing to
worry about. Death is just like going to sleep and waking up
at once in heaven. It's like just stepping over the road to the
other side."

"Well, thank you Billy. You can go now."

"But, Mister Albright, Sir. Have you given your heart to Jesus? Do you know you are going to heaven?"

"Guess I sure hope so, Billy. Don't forget I'm a deacon in
my church. Done a lot of good things too, you know. I mean
where would you be today if it were not for me, eh Billy? And
there's also my parents and Ernestine's. Good people. All of
them. I even have my name mounted on that corner plate of the
new education building at the church. Wife and I gave a ton for

that one. Glad too. Preacher and I are good friends, too. And one other thing, I..."

Billy Bob interrupted his boss.

"But, Mister Albright, Sir, you and I both know we're about to die. It is very important that..."

"That will be enough Billy!" Rhodes reacted. One thing he did not tolerate was insolence. Especially from an insubordinate. A gardener at that!

"Leave me alone!"

Six

Within two days Albright's condition had taken a turn for the worse. At times he would not speak for hours. It was like he had withdrawn into a shell. He became confused and disoriented. Harry came by the estate almost every day. He told Ernestine the cancer had a grade of about nine. Bad. Real bad, he said.

"Need to make him as comfortable as possible, now Nesty," he said as he put a loving arm around her.

"Talk to me, Harry. Tell me like it is. What can we expect?"

Dr. Taylor realized there was no sense in avoiding the issue. It would be far better for her to be prepared so she could anticipate things. He pulled up a chair in the spacious living room. Awards and trophies of every kind adorned the walls. Special recognitions clamored for their rightful place on the walls of fame. The stuffed heads of every kind of exotic animal bore testimony to numerous safaris undertaken to the plains of Africa and far away places.

Sue Ellen entered, tea tray in hand. She had served the doctor many times and understood just how much he loved a good cup of English Breakfast Tea served in her mistress' best china tea cups. She, too, had a deep affection and appreciation for the doctor. He always treated her like a lady and showed her a great deal of respect. Harry liked his tea with real milk and added a small spoon of sugar to accommodate his sweet tooth. Lifting the cup through the use of his thumb and index finger had become an art envied by many an admirer. It was no wonder he and his wife could often be seen taking afternoon tea at the Windsor Court Hotel. Their good friends the Pounds', the Kelley's, the Stevens', and even the Foley's would join them there and make for a delightful afternoon.

Tea aside, Harry knew the business at hand was very serious.

"Well, Nesty, I'm not sure if you will be very comfortable with the details but I do realize it is better for you to know the facts. Please remember that each person can respond differently. Certainly, in the case of my friend, I would hope for as little suffering as possible. Be assured I will do my part. I know you will do yours. But I cannot do any less than tell you that this form of cancer could be accompanied by some very difficult days for both you and your husband."

"Albright will gradually get to the point where he will no longer be able to empty his bladder. I know he is already getting up more than several times at night. In some cases, the prostate cancer will completely close off the urethra. The urethra, of course, which empties the bladder, passes right through the prostate before passing out of the body. In many cases, the prostate starts bleeding, especially in the late stages. By then the patient is already typically anemic and his pain and discomfort level is rendering him immobile. As we have already noticed weight loss becomes a serious thing to observe."

He took another sip of tea so as to make certain Ernestine had not heard enough. She sat very still. Both hands were delicately placed on her lap as she sat up straight on the front end of the sofa.

"The problem of bleeding originates in the prostate gland because it completely replaces the normal prostate tissue. The blood vessel walls erode through thus causing blood to gush forth. Typically the patient is already fairly or relatively malnourished and may not have good clotting factors. And a lower threshold for bleeding. Blood oozes back into the bladder and then settles in the bottom of the bladder. When, and I might add Nesty, if, this happens to Albright, a blood clot will form in the bladder. I will tell you this condition can be very painful. It will make Al very miserable indeed."

"Do you think this is likely in Al's case, Harry?" By now her apparent stoicism had changed to an obvious consternation.

"Should this happen, Nesty, we will take him to surgery and cystoscope him under anesthesia in order to wash out his bladder and try to cauterize all the bleeders in the prostate we can find. At this point, he will not be a candidate for open surgery. Typically at this stage he would be in the most untenable position because of the pain associated with an inability to urinate. Basically the best we can do for Al, at this point, is to make him comfortable. And I must alert you, Nesty, that it is possible Al will become so malnourished he will loose dramatic amounts of weight. The reason I tell you this is to prepare you, Nesty. And I would let the kids know too. Patients like this become so emaciated they look like skeletons. This can be very frightening, especially for the kids and grandkids. So it's better to heads up with them. And I would recommend a hospice nurse right away. You cannot do this alone, Nesty."

"What will actually cause him to die, Harry?" she whispered hesitatingly.

"Typically, if we can get him to Oschner Hospital we will dose him heavily with intravenous morphine to the point to where he will be sort of semi-conscious and barely coherent. He could die of anemia, dehydration or, perhaps cardiac arrest brought on by his chronic anemic situation. In some cases, some of our patients have died from uremic poisoning. We call that acute renal failure. This is caused by the on-going growth of the cancer to the point at which it replaces the prostate, closes off the urethra, but also grows up into the base of the bladder where the openings to the ureters are situated. These ureters are the tubes that drain the kidneys and connect to the bladder. But this kind of situation sometimes takes a long time to develop. If the kidneys are obstructed the patient will die of kidney failure. Not a bad way to die, I might add, because as his creatinine gets higher and higher the patient becomes comatose. In a way he will just drift off. Kind of like going to sleep. That's why I said it is a more pleasant way to die. Not that there is any good way to die, Nesty."

Within the week Albright was writhing in pain. At times he would be so confused it was hard to make sense out of anything he was saying. A steady stream of visitors stood at his bedside. Hospice nurses gave him round the clock care and his family increasingly settled into hushed huddles of conversation and deep inner reflection.

As Albright lay there his mind began to take journeys into dark and horrible places. He was basically unable to talk. Some called it hallucinations; others likened it to a man crying out in the middle of a dream. At times he heard the most horrible sounds coming from the darkest pits he had ever seen. It reminded him of some of the terror movies he had bought for the grand kids during Halloween.

One of the favorite times of the year for the grand parents was late October. Bebo, as they called him, took great care to dress as the ugliest monster imaginable. The kids would run all over the house screaming while trying to find places of refuge. Ernestine's favorite costume was the one that transformed her into a real live witch. A shop on Veterans' Boulevard stocked a face more hideous than hideous ever was described. Then they would all dress up as demons and monsters and such and go out into the Garden District "trick or treating." Not to mention the haunted houses, cobwebs, tombstones and stuff.

But these things had taken a strange turn now. The fun was gone. Games were over. Albright's moans and screams bore audible testimony to the agony of his soul.

"Don't think it will be much longer, now," Doctor Huey opined. He felt cardiac arrest was a definite possibility. Rhodes's vital signs were slipping. Taylor concurred.

Time was lost in a never ending search for freedom. Nothing else seemed to have any value anymore. Not even the business. Not even the kids. Nothing.

From time to time he appeared to come around. The pastor would hold his hand and say good things, mostly for the benefit of the family. Expressions of gratitude poured in through the front door. Flowers arrived in vases, bouquets and in every other form imaginable. So many cards made their way to the Rhodes' estate the postal service boxed them in through the delivery entrance. They wished Albright well, voiced many expressions of gratitude for his life of generosity, and contained beautiful prayers for a full and complete recovery. Best of all were the hand drawn pictures which adorned the walls of his spacious suite.

The one he loved most simply read, "I love you Bebo. You're the best Bebo in the world! Love Ally."

Out of all the grand kids Ally was his favorite. He'd taught him all about the greatest values in life. Like "working hard," "making money work for you," "never letting your guard down," and "making your Bebo proud."

Early one Thursday morning, after a sleepless night, Albright felt himself drifting into that kind of neither here nor there kind of sleep. He was aware of his room. The hospice nurse sat in her usual chair, available at a moment's notice. Ernestine's reassuring voice seemed ever present, even though she had retired to her own bedroom to catch up on lost sleep. The bed sheets had been changed and rearranged many times but still clung to him. Every crease seemed glued to his body as he shifted and turned while chained to the intravenous tubes which ran out of his arms.

Bags of medicines and morphine hung silently on their stands peering down at their pathetic target like a squadron of metal matchstick men sworn to silence and secrecy.

At first he wasn't quite sure who they were. Maybe he didn't want to know. They stood still and yet moved like shadows in the wind. It was like they were waiting for him. It scared the dickens out of him. Albright shifted in his bed and felt the distinct twitch of nerves in his stomach. He sensed something major was about to happen and they had something to do with whatever it was.

He could feel the sweat running down his neck. All of a sudden they came at him out of the shadows. Dark rays like ultra-violet light illuminated their faces. Monsters. Hideous creature-like monsters. They were awful, frightening, cunning, salivating like a pack of jackals.

Albright screamed but nobody seemed to listen. He called out to Ernestine but when he turned to find her she was gone. Then he realized where he was.

He was standing in a huge, dark valley. Massive mountain ranges surrounded him at every point. Dark clouds rumbled and roared across the sky before slamming headlong into the sides of the mountains. The resulting collisions sent boom after boom of gut wrenching thunder back down the mountain slopes with such force that Rhodes was hurled head over heels into the hardened earth and towards the oncoming demon monsters.

As he tumbled he grabbed every blade of grass and tuft of weed in the hopes of preventing the inevitable. But nothing could stem the force with which he was being delivered to the monsters. Just as he ran into their open arms he felt the hospice nurse mop his brow with a damp cloth.

Great relief filled his heart and soul. His pastor was standing at the end of the bed with an arm over the shoulder of Ernestine. Both Taylor and Huey were there too. Albright thought he could hear their muffled conversation. But it was more muffled than a conversation.

"Won't be much longer, Nesty."

"Is he suffering, Harry?" she asked in a desperate attempt to be reassured her husband was not hurting.

"Hard to say," came the reply.

"We've given him 'bout all the morphine he can take. At least he's comfortable. Systems shutting down rather quickly now. William thinks his heart will give in like we discussed. God'll take care of him."

"Yeh," said Rothy with tears streaming down his cheeks.

"God's sure gonna like having someone run the business up there!"

They all smiled through their pain. The pastor asked them all to join hands and pray. Nobody argued.

Albright heard the first part. Something about Jesus loaning him to earth for seventy-nine years or something.

But there they were again. Just standing there in the shadows. Albright was dressed in his pajamas which kind of made him feel uncomfortable. Every member of the Rhodes family could be seen standing at the windows of the home. The one on the estate. Not the one on the farm in East Texas but the one in the Garden District of New Orleans. They all looked pale and ashen. Some were crying. But most had sullen, somewhat blank expressions on their faces.

He tried to call out to them but they just carried on like they weren't even aware of his predicament. His two sons, Amby and Rothy, came into view with heavy bags of money strapped to their shoulders. They proceeded to pluck large bundles of cash out of the shoulder bags. Wads and wads of bright green one hundred dollar bills. Stacks and stacks of them. Albright clearly could see the bills themselves as the boys piled them up in the house. What caught his eye was the caption just under The United States of America. It read "In God We Trust." God, he thought, where is God? In desperation he looked around the valley in which he found himself. The creatures were still there. Standing. Waiting.

He spun around fixing his attention on the activities of his home and family. There was so much money it began to stick out of the windows and doors. Several hundred wads began to pour out of the chimney just above the living room. What he saw next appalled him. Amby and Rothy walked outside and began to dig a huge hole with a backhoe. They emptied thousands of one hundred dollar bills into the hole and covered it up. The two brothers shook hands and went back inside.

"Our secret," the elder said to the younger. "Any rate, they won't miss a few million. Come on, let's go take care of the rest of the family. Daddy would want it this way, anyway!"

Amby and his brother entered through the back door of the mansion without having noticed their every move had been observed by their house maid. Sue Ellen simply shook her head and retreated to her little home behind the hedges.

"How's my sweetie pie?" she asked tenderly of her husband. He rolled his eyes to meet her gaze. His body was emaciated. The disease had done its dirty work. She reached out and took his skeletal hands in hers and began to stroke them so softly one would have thought they were on their first date.

His voice cracked in response. "The Lord Jesus is so good, Sweetness. How is Mister Albright doing? I am so concerned about him. Wish and pray he would give his heart to Jesus!"

Seven

Back in Albright's bedroom a gathering was taking place. The doctors had concurred. It was time to summon the entire family. All of them, including the grandchildren, their pastor, the Reverend Benjamin Franks, the hospice nurses, Doctors Taylor and Huey were assembled in their Daddy's room.

His color had changed to a ghostly shade of grey. His mouth hung open and his eyes were at half mast. Closer observation revealed a blank stare. The tubes that ran in and out of his mouth slowly carried their liquid cargo back and forth in reluctant obedience to machines that demanded their attention. Other pipes and tubes discharged their wares in bags placed delicately under the bed so as to provide maximum discreetness.

They all thought he was dead. But the periodic rise and fall of his chest confirmed the vestiges of a man desperately clinging to life. On at least one occasion he seemed to open his eyes as though pleading for someone to help him. On other occasions Albright muttered and moaned leaving the distinct impression he was either in agony or was engaged in some kind of nightmare.

The dying man, though, was not in the room. His body was, for sure, but he found himself staring back at the home from his position in the valley. It was like he was having a bad dream.

Albright could hardly believe his own sons would be so deceitful. For a moment he just stood there and watched. Even he was appalled. His two sons proceeded to hand out wads of dollar bills to the rest of the family. The sisters seemed content. The grand kids were delighted. Ernestine just stood and watched without comment. Albright tried to protest but nothing came out of his mouth. It was his money, he thought. What do they think they are doing with my money? But the distraction with the goings on at his home was suddenly interrupted by the creatures. He had totally forgotten about them. They were still chasing him.

He spun around just in time to see them coming at a gallop towards him. The money was suddenly forgotten. He had to run. Hard and fast. So he began to run. Fast. Real fast. He set his sights on the mountain cliffs up ahead. The ones that loomed over the valley. The ones that sent peals of thunderclaps cascading down their sides like a defeated army on the run from a victorious, yet vengeful opponent seeking to wreak havoc on the vanquished.

But it seemed the faster he ran and the harder he tried the closer they came. It was like the hundred yard dash at the Olympic Games being seen in super slow motion. The faster he ran the slower he seemed to go. The monster creatures gained with every stride. Terror gripped his heart and soul. He had to escape. He had to get away. He had to find somewhere to escape. He began to scream. His pajamas flapped and flopped in the wind. One of the creatures stretched out an arm towards the panic stricken Albright Rhodes.

It had finger nails which protruded from beneath the most hideous looking gnarled hand he had ever laid his eyes on. A vile cackling sound emanated from within the beast. Other creatures joined the unlikely chorus to the point at which their hideous sounds ricocheted off the walls of the towering mountains. Their disgusting vibrations joined forces with the already deafening thunder claps which repeatedly cascaded down into the valley thus forming an unholy matrimony of vile and obscene noise which penetrated the eardrums of the fleeing man. His eardrums burst in his ears sending acute pain down through his anatomy and all the way to the final outposts of his toes. So sharp was the pain that even his toe nails split apart. As they did so they rose up from within the toe and began to separate themselves from the skin which clung desperately to their protective covering. The skin and the nail were ripped apart like a tortoise being ripped out of its shell.

Now the man could no longer hear but he kept on running. His bare feet squirted long jets of blood from his ruptured toes as he stretched every muscle in his body in an effort to evade the outstretched arm of the hideous creature.

Too late! One of the finger nails caught the top collar of his blue stripped pajamas. Before Albright could even register a protest he was rendered completely naked, his covering having been torn from his fleeing torso. Propelled by the abject terror of his situation he sprinted even harder than before. For a man who had seldom been seen in a bathing suit, let alone stark naked, his presentation mortified him. Out the corner of his eye he tried to see if any of the family were watching his humiliation. But they seemed oblivious.

The base of the mountain range presented itself to the fugitive. He stole a fleeting glance over his right shoulder and was relieved to note the creatures had paused, either to gather their wits, discuss new strategies, or simply gloat over the acquisition of the Chief Executive Officer's blue stripped pajamas. At least one of them had the unlikely prize raised above his head and was waving it like the flag of a victorious field regiment in the American Civil War while the defeated enemy ran for their lives.

Albright had cried out so many times Ernestine had taken up station alongside his bed, damp cloth in hand. As she gently mopped his brow Albright vaguely became aware of her presence.

He reached out a feeble hand which was quickly restrained by the hospice nurse and one of the other specialists he had flown in from Chicago.

"Help me," he pleaded in a weak delirious voice. "Please, help me!"

"It's O.K., Al, we're all here with you. The whole family."

"We love you Daddy, don't worry. We're here Daddy. It'll be alright, I promise you."

Rhodes tried to respond. He wanted to tell them about the creatures. Somehow he had to warn them. But just as he began to articulate he found himself looking up at the towering peaks in front of him.

The monsters had resumed their pursuit. Albright desperately took hold of one of the ledges in the rock face and began hauling himself up the sheer cliff face one foot, one grip at a time. He dared not look down. For one thing heights had never sat well with his constitution. And, to be quite frank, he had no interest in trying to define the progress of the creatures. He could hear them and that was quite sufficient motivation. Up and up he climbed. Higher and higher. One ledge to the next. He was exhausted in every way. Both hands had been cut and mangled by the sharp edges of the rock face. The front side of his naked anatomy looked like a mosaic of bleeding patterns oozing with blood.

"Please, let me wake up from this nightmare," he pleaded with himself.

But the nightmare continued. Sweat poured from his body as he lay in his bed. The periodic lapses between each faltering gasp for breath became longer and longer so that those who gathered around him frequently thought he was gone.

Much to his relief he finally made it to the top of the mountain. He hauled himself up and over the final protrusion and lay momentarily in a pitiful heap of thorough exhaustion. His senses harnessed themselves together in order of cohesiveness making it possible for him to gather his thoughts. Slowly he dragged his aching body to its feet and was somewhat relieved to notice the creatures had disappeared. Further observation revealed not only the massive cliffs he had just traversed but the valley below where he had first encountered the creatures. Way in the distance he could distinguish his home. The family was still standing at each window and wads of money seemed to be everywhere. He called out to them but they seemed not to pay any attention.

His obvious predicament lay in his quest to return to his loved ones. The creatures seemed to have vanished and he realized the arduous, but necessary task that lay ahead of him, if he was to climb back down the cliffs.

But the sounds of their horrendous chatter came back with vengeance. Their proximity puzzled him. They stood together on the far side of the summit. How they had gotten there, he knew not.

One of them suddenly took off. The smallest pair of wings adorned its back and buzzed like a chainsaw at work in the forests of Child's Play, the family ranch in Texas. The others followed suit as though summoned by their commanding officer. The combined pitch produced by multiple little wings all buzzing in unison sent volley after volley of earth-shattering sound cascading over the cliffs of the mountainside. The whole earth rumbled in response while numerous rocks and stones ran from their presence in a vain effort to hide from their impending judgment.

Albright A. Rhodes froze in abject terror. He had nowhere to go. No place to hide. It was over.

In a desperate, though futile effort to obliterate their advancing presence, he turned his back on them.

The house was just standing there in the valley below. Way down there. It seemed like it was fading in the mist as it overlooked the most beautiful of all lakes. It reminded him of that movie about Indians filmed in Chimney Rock, North Carolina. He remembered how the family would spend glorious days in the cabin at Lake Lure surrounded by such majestic glory. It was there they would all gather to watch The Last of the Mohicans. Albright stood at the very sight where the girl had chosen to hurl herself over the cliff instead of being taken captive by the mean man who stood before her. Albright knew exactly what he needed to do. Now it was his turn. Without much further thought the owner of Texas Mete jumped.

The strangest thing happened, though. As his body careened down the side of the mountain there was a rushing sound like the air being let out of a balloon. It seemed like he was floating. Even flying in a way. Creatures appeared on each side of him, but they did not touch him. They simply smiled hideously. Then the air stopped and he landed gently on the ground.

Ernestine saw it before the rest of the group. She called out and everyone could hear the desperation in her broken voice.

Albright's eyes were wide open. He was trying to say something but, by now, the family had grown accustomed to his sounds. His chest heaved and his mouth opened. It was as though he was taking one final drink of life giving air. Just one more for the journey. Ernestine held his hand and cried out.

Harry put a finger on his friend's neck. Then he leaned over him while the nurse searched for a pulse.

"I'm afraid he's gone!"

Ernestine's tears flowed. She leaned over and kissed her husband on the forehead. One by one the family came. Their grief was extreme. They had lost their Daddy and Bebo. He was seventy-nine years of age and had lived a full, good life.

Albright suddenly realized he was trapped. The struggle was over. The creatures had him surrounded. One of them stepped forward and began to chain him up. Wrists, arms, body, ankles, legs. He tried to protest but in vain. A wagon-like vehicle drove up to where he was standing. It was packed with other people. He was shoved up into the last seat at the back end. As it began to move off he just barely could make out the form of his home as it rapidly was swallowed up in the mist. The driver drove on.

PART III

THE RICH MAN DIED AND WAS BURIED. IN
HELL HE LIFTED UP HIS EYES, BEING IN
TORMENT, AND SAW THE POOR MAN IN THE
BOSOM OF ABRAHAM.

One

A s Albright arrived at the massive gated entrance he considered himself fortunate, in a strange sort of way, to have
been placed in the final seat of the large wagon-like vehicle. He
still was not sure if it was a Ford or Chevy truck but it wouldn't
have made any difference anyway. He'd always preferred the
Ford truck.

The six armed creatures that provided their escort did not
seem too concerned about the prisoners' basic comforts. Even
though the sign outside had placed a clear limitation on the seating capacity, twenty-eight people had been unceremoniously
herded into the back of this thing. At least four of them had become jammed under the seating which was simply a plank that
stretched from the driver's cab to the tail gate of the wagon.

As shocked as he was Albright tried to stand up to give his seat to one of the older ladies he noticed desperately trying to hold on to anything that would help her. Her chubby arms fanned around like a bird with a broken wing trying to stay in the sky. The stern warning his father-in-law, Landrum Rothschild, had given him that day on the farm, had never been forgotten. Even in his later years people would often comment on just how well cultured and mannered he had always been.

As he tried to stand up he discovered he could not do so. He thought it must have been the chains but, upon further observation, he was not chained to the floor or plank in any way. He just couldn't do it. So he sat there and watched in horror as these two elderly ladies crumbled with exhaustion and looked as though they were about to collapse. But they just didn't seem to have the ability to fall over which would have made it a little better for them. Two of the others who were trapped under the bench seats began to scream in pain. One person, in particular, caught Albright's eye.

He was none other than the Senator from New York. Senator James P. Zondervan had been the majority leader in the Senate and was widely considered one of the most likely candidates to succeed President Gallen P. Sutcliffe when his term expired. He had hit the campaign trail hard and aggressively, covering as many as ten States in a day on some occasions. His war chest was considerable, which was no wonder when one took into account his incredible speaking ability. When he took New Hampshire by as much as twenty percent over the next Republican hopeful many believed his nomination was a lock. Even though he himself was a true Southerner, Mister Rhodes liked Sutcliffe's political agenda, especially on the matters of social security and the fiscal responsibility. Rhodes had voted all the way for Sutcliffe but was always a little miffed when he "wore his religion" on his shoulder too much.

"That's what got President Cantrell into trouble", he would lecture his boys.

A vote for a Northerner, let alone a Yankee, would ensure another four years of the Oval Office. Nothing was deemed more critical than to have the White House in the right hands.

What are you doing here, Senator?" he inquired.

"Snow storm in Montana, Albright", he replied. "Pilot told us it would go over our heads. The idiot. Caught the tail end of it. Down we went like a ton of bricks. Right in the middle of my campaign. Talk about an upset! What a nuisance. Who are these horrid looking creatures? Where are they taking us?"

Albright shifted uneasily. He turned his head to the outside and peered through the crack in the canvas that covered the back of the truck.

Two

His family was still standing around his bed. He could see them there. It puzzled him for a split second but he was still there with his family. What a relief!

Ernestine had him by the hand and was stroking his forehead with some kind of cloth. Tears flowed down her cheeks. What really got to him were the children. There stood Amby, tall and dark, accomplished in every way. He had always been his daddy's favorite. Now he was the Chief Executive Officer of Texas Mete, an accomplishment which had made Albright so happy at one stage. But it was different now. Things had changed, somehow.

His other son Rothy still struggled. The money, the condos and the shares his father had left to him in his will were designed to pull him straight. Money always made the difference. Albright knew that much. His own life was the best example.

But something was different now. One of his sons-in-law had put on so much weight there wasn't a single chair in the room big enough to accommodate his massive frame. Netty, his daughter, who went by the name of Natalie, was not much smaller either. She and her sister Rosemary stood side by side howling with grief. Word had not gotten to Rose's estranged husband, Sean, who was probably out womanizing as usual. All Rose seemed to be able to say was "Daddy, daddy, daddy! Please don't leave me Daddy!"

There they were. His entire family. All of them crying and some so distraught the nurse was asked to administer tranquilizers. Even his mother-in-law had to be wheeled out of the room in the wheel chair Albright had ordered especially for her from Johnson manufacturers in Wilton, Connecticut.

Albright shifted nervously. By some strange phenomenon he was staring at the senator from New York again. But then he was also able to see every detail of the room he was lying in at home. He shook his head hoping to clear his mind, but to no avail. Here he was in the back of this miserable truck surrounded by horrible creatures, listening to the screams of the prisoners around him, but at the same time he was in bed surrounded by his family.

From the vantage point of his seat at the back of the wagon he watched in mystified horror as his mother-in-law went into cardiac arrest. The same blue lights he had seen just a few minutes earlier began to flash in the hallways of Baptist Hospital right there on Napoleon Street. It was only a few blocks from the Rhodes estate.

He shouted out to Nesty's mother. He desperately wanted to insist she turn her life over to Jesus Christ because a gradual realization began to flood his mind. But she didn't seem to be paying much attention. Her eyes protruded from their sockets and gave her a look of panic and desperation. Medical personnel swarmed around her like a colony of mad army ants bent on the destruction of a neighboring colony. The doctors literally ripped her blouse off the front of her body. Then she was picked up and placed on a table which stood silently in the hall way. With desperate motion they wheeled her into the adjoining surgery room where the doctor took hold of the two shock pads and laid them on her exposed chest. On the count of three a massive current of electricity was applied to her heart zone but Albright realized it was too late.

He saw a troop of the same creatures fly by the wagon he was in. They were dressed in a black garb and carried the same documents they had shown him when they came for him at the house. They also had the large sign. It certainly resembled the one they had brought into his room. The one they had brought into his bedroom had his name printed in big black letters. But this time her name was painted on it. The lettering was bold and unmistakable.

As he watched the unfolding of events taking place in the hospital where Nesty's mother was dying, Rhodes found himself recalling his own experience. For just a brief moment he relived the moment when the creatures showed up. When they arrived at Albright's bedside accompanied by all the groaning and growling they did, it made Rhodes think, just for a second, that he was dreaming. He had flown into airports all over the world and always had a number of immaculately dressed people standing at the gateway with a large board or document bearing his name. Albright A. Rhodes never had to hail a cab or carry his own luggage, even when he flew commercial.

This time it was not quite the same, however. These creatures had a great deal of armor all over their bodies and their faces were hideous. Rhodes could hardly look at them. They looked like demon angels and made Rhodes think of some of the comic books he and his wife had always bought for the grand kids, especially when they were on vacation. The kids also had a huge video game collection. Their favorite was called "Dungeons and Dragons". Albright winced as he looked at the grotesque faces of the creatures because they reminded him of the creatures in Dungeons and Dragons. Somehow he wished he had never allowed his grand kids to be exposed to such evil beings—even if it was just a game. As he recoiled in horror one of them caught Albright's eye. His mouth opened as if to say something but instead of words coming out a single flame of fire shot out between the gaps in his contorted face.

Mister Rhodes cried out to his family but they seemed not to pay him any attention. It was like he was in another world. His whole body ached. He figured it must be all the drugs and medicine he was being given. Of course he trusted the panel of specialists. Most of them had been life long friends and he had flown the best of them down to New Orleans to take care of him. He pulled at the chain around his neck because it was so tight. As he did so it cut deeply into his skin to the point at which the pain became unbearable. The wagon kept on driving.

Three

In horror he watched Ernestine drop to her knees as the doctor came in to tell her about her mother. It was just as well the grand kids were in the visitor's room drinking cokes brought to them by their maid Sue Ellen. This was all too much.

Then he watched as they came and tried to pry his hands from those of his family. Rosemary screamed in reluctance as the medical personnel nudged her away. The chaplain kept saying "bless y'all," until Rothy spun around and told him to "shut up your face!" in no uncertain terms. Embarrassed, he slipped quietly into the corner of the room.

A nurse pulled the sheet right over his head. But he was watching. He caught himself trying to pull the sheet away from his face but then, realized he was riding in this wagon. Next minute two men in black suits came in and put him on a roller thing and wheeled him out to a parked car that sure resembled a hearse. At the mortuary they left him lying on this slab of concrete without a pillow or anything to cover his nakedness. He had lost all his personal dignity. Some fellow with a white coat took a knife and began to cut open his entire chest. There was no anesthetic applied either. The doctor-looking person kept stopping to write down all the things he saw inside the abdomen. Then he put suctions and tubes in every opening of his body so that Albright felt as though everything was just draining out of him.

A huge bump in the road caused all the people in the wagon to yell out in pain. For just a second Albright looked away from all they were doing to him down there at Kelley's Funeral Home. Oddly, he felt no pain from what they were doing to his body. The pain he was experiencing was right there in the wagon. The chains. He felt like he was choking to death but he couldn't die. Maybe he was dead and just didn't know it.

Four

Back at the Rhodes Estate the whole family gathered. What really annoyed Albright were the numbers of people who turned up to give comfort to his wife. Some of them were genuine but some were after his money. It was strange. He had never been able to do this before. Not only could he listen to every conversation at the same time, but he could hear and understand every thought and motive. This really ticked him off.

Especially when Charles W. Guidrot turned up. What was he doing there?

Guidrot was another major rival in the business world. Turkle Hot Sauce seemed to have held the number one spot on the world market forever, even though Tabasco was widely regarded as their main rival. To make matters worse the relationship between the Rhodes' clan and the Guidrots was chilly at best.

Here he was with his arm around Ernestine. His own wife had passed on after a tumultuous marriage during which she had to deal with her husband's infidelity times without number.

Rhodes could read his mind. The little weasel! Marry Ernestine and hey presto! Did Guidrot think he was a fool or something? And well he knew Nesty was still an extremely attractive lady. Slim, trim with the look of one of those beautiful southern ladies. Her skin was like silk and her petite mouth shone when she smiled. Back in his bedroom Rose and Netty were dividing up his suits, sports' jackets and things.

"Dadgumit!" he muttered.

There were the usual loads of food catered by La Madeleine down near the river front. And because of the large crowd the family had asked the catering service from Copelands' Restaurant to do a special lay out for them. They particularly wanted Albright's favorites to be included in the menu. So, one look at the banquet table revealed broccoli balls with plenty of the mouth watering dip sauce, ricochet catfish, loads of blackened gulf red fish, shrimp ducky and blackened shrimp and several other specialties. The sea food gumbo was served out of the late Mrs. Rothschild's huge pure silver bowl. They knew this would please Albright.

The kids ran around outside. He also noticed how the oldest grandson, Ally, named for Albright, of course, had spotted a rather attractive little girl and was making advances towards her.

"Way to go, boy!" he muttered to himself without noticing that the wagon had turned and was headed straight up the side of a mountain cliff face.

Five

Sue Ellen was running around cleaning up the mess while trying to tend to her very sick husband at the same time. Just as well Albright had always kept them hidden behind the row of trees at the back end of the mansion.

Suddenly he saw himself lying in this box all dressed up in his pin stripe suit. For a long time, which seemed no time to him, scores and scores of people walked slowly by. They stopped and he would find himself staring up into faces which were peering down at him. Then they said the nicest of things to him. Many just said nothing. Others talked about all he had done for the community, the new libraries he had built, the support he had given to all the political candidates, and the thousands of acres of land he had donated to the State so as to protect the wildlife. It seemed that none of these things were quite so important to him anymore. But he still couldn't understand why.

Six

In the wagon it didn't seem to matter any more. The climb up the mountain side came to an end. The wagon came to an abrupt halt. The back of the wagon flew open and the creatures began to manhandle the prisoners out of it. One of the young men tripped and fell headlong onto the ground. The back of the wagon was about ten feet high. The boy's neck snapped as he hit the dirt. All the prisoners could hear his bones break. It sounded like small firecrackers popping during July fourth festivities in the park out at Kenner. What terrified them all was how the young man stumbled to his feet and kept walking with his broken neck and all.

In front of them loomed the largest iron gate Albright had ever seen. And that was saying something considering all the security fences and gates and alarm systems he had installed around his properties to protect his family. He could even remember when he lost his temper with Sue Ellen's husband, Billy Bob. That was the day those two big dogs had broken through the guard fence of the estate and had eaten all the choice lamb cuts which had been set out for his prize Welsh Corgis.

Despite being literally "chewed out" Billy Bob just stood there with his head slightly bent down as though he was standing before a mighty king. The man was so humble it drove Albright insane! Particularly the old man's incessant whistling and singing of hymns. Sounded like he was stuck on "Amazing grace how sweet the sound, that saved a wretch like me. I once was lost but now I'm found, I was blind but now I see."

But for his secret obligation to the girl Albright would have ordered him off his property.

Deep down he knew this was a funeral he was observing. He wanted to cry, or scream, or shout. It took place at the big church.

"Please just tell them the truth!" he screamed to no avail.

The creatures herded them like cattle to the front section outside the big iron gate. Albright looked around. He nearly choked when he saw his own mother-in-law standing in chains in the section next to his. She looked different. She was mouthing something to him. It was so hard to concentrate but then he realized what she was saying.

"We're dead! It's too late, Albright!"

Albright A. Rhodes suddenly went cold. Then hot. Extremely hot. He tried to cry out but nothing would come out of his mouth.

Next minute one of the creatures stood before them arrayed in magnificent black armor.

"Ladies and gentlemen. I am Hogwarts. I am supreme commander of the royal order of Beelzebub. I have under my command legions of angels. We are loyal only to our Lord Beelzebub. His wish is our command. He alone is the Alpha and the Omega. He alone is the beginning and the end. We are here to worship him for all time and all eternity."

"Ladies and gentlemen. I give you His Royal Highness Lucifer Beelzebub the first of Babylon. Mighty in power, Lord of all the universe. The one whose triumph over Jehovah is assured. Ladies and gentlemen, put your faces to the ground and let there be silence in the kingdom!"

The thousands upon thousands of chained prisoners fell to the ground as one man. Thunder and lightening sounded forth from the abyss. The earth upon which they lay seemed to open at its core. From deep within there arose a sound like mighty rushing wind. Everything began to shake with a violence Albright had not seen even in Iwo Jima. There he had witnessed death's horrors first hand. It was there he had vowed to strive for the peace of the world. It was there he made a pledge to "put his money where his mouth is." It was during those terrible days of war and supreme sacrifice he had seen with his own eyes the inhumanity of man to man.

But the sounds of violence that ushered in this hideous monster were unlike anything he had ever imagined. Colossal plumes of fire leaped forth from the bowels of the earth causing the entire stratosphere to be set ablaze. Molten lava gushed forth by the tons and began to wrap its blazing fangs around the legs of the prisoners like the circulating skin of a huge anaconda. The burning of their flesh was accompanied by the sounds of a discombobulated orchestra of screams and cries for help. While their flesh burned the shape of their feet and the contours of their skin remained intact and unchanged. It was like they were burning and yet they were not.

Seven

A s the earth began to shake the legions of angels raised their swords and shields in unison. With their lances they pounded on their shields causing a rhythmic sound like Shaka Zulu's warrior Impis preparing to go into the battle at Blood River against the Afrikaner commandos known as the Boers.

The deafening thump of sword on shield built up into a crescendo so loud it burst the eardrums of every prisoner in chains. Albright felt his left ear drum explode first. Then the second burst so violently he thought the whole right side of his face had been removed. He looked sideways very quickly so as not to offend one of the creatures and noticed the others with stuff oozing out of their ears. And yet he continued to hear every sound. Every deafening syllable. Every word. Every command.

Suddenly he could see a massive structure begin to rise slowly from the depths of the earth. At first glance it looked like the Washington Memorial in D.C.. Straight, powerful and immense. On the top most point of this towering mass of concrete was a throne so splendid it made all the prisoners want to cover their eyes. The seat was made of pure gold and was covered with what seemed to be the skins of a thousand sheep. The arms were solid ivory and the legs were made of yellow wood that looked like it came from the Tzitzikama Forests of South Africa.

The one who was seated on the throne was more horrible and hideous than the worst of nightmares. His feet were webbed together and covered in what looked like the massive scales of a monster fish. Each toe was uniquely fitted with a toe nail that looked more like one of Shaka Zulu's assegai stabbing spears than a human nail. His knees were contorted and gnarled. His pelvic region was a mangled fusion between male and female. On his chest he wore an insignia that hailed his undisputed lordship over the universe.

The inscription read: "FATHER OF LIES."

His head bore testimony to at least eight eyes. Two in front, two on each side and two on the back. As Albright stared in horror at this beast he had the distinct impression he could see everything at all times. Each side of his face produced a twisted nose. On his head he wore a brilliant crown made up of thousands of diamonds. As each plume of fire catapulted out of the abyss the diamonds glittered in brilliant glory. His mouth was the most awful of all his features. It was just a hideous gap. Inside were to be found every ghastly reptile known to man.

Hogwarts held up both arms. There was silence.

Slowly and deliberately His Royal Majesty stood to his feet.

"I am Lucifer Beelzebub the first of Babylon. I am because I am the great I am. Do not be deceived. There is none other. I alone am the first and the last. From the day of my existence, not even Jehovah could contain me. He is within my grasp. I am the father of all nations. All people will bow down and worship just as you have already done. You, ladies and gentlemen, are the evidence of my almighty power. You are the demonstration of my presence. You have spent your lives serving me as millions have done before you and millions more will do before I march against Jehovah on that great day. Without me you can do nothing. You are my slaves forever.

"I have instructed my right hand, Hogwarts, to make preparation for battle. It began the day I took control in the garden. It has already been set in course. My plan is to control the mind of man. I use whatever is necessary. Political constitutions, politicians, preachers, priests, power and individual potential. I use them all. I prowl the streets seeking whom I may devour. I infiltrate the minds of feeble people through the clever use of the books they read, the movies they watch and the deep rooted feelings they have. I am the one who seeks, devours and destroys. I am the eternal terminator. Just when they think I'm gone I'll be back. Just when they think they have gotten rid of me I show up. There I am. I am in their bedrooms. I am in their desires. I am behind their motives. I am in their children. I demonstrate against law, order and justice. Everything that is built up I tear down. I use them. Their money, their fame, their fortune, their greed, their lust. I am lust, I am greed, I am fame, I am fortune. Ever since I was summarily dismissed from heaven I have determined to prove, once and for all, who is king of the universe!

"Ladies and gentlemen, behold your king! This is my kingdom and you are my slaves forever. Welcome to eternal hell!"

And with that Lucifer Beelzebub the first of Babylon vanished from their eyes.

Hogwarts stepped forward. The pride in his horrid eyes glowed to the point at which a greenish-blue liquid began to ooze from each eye and dribble down onto his chest. As he raised his spear legions of demon angels flew here and there shouting curses and screaming blood curdling insults at the prisoners.

"Worship the beast! Worship the beast! Worship the beast"

Hogwarts raised his spear once again and silence fell upon their ears. Then in a loud voice he cried, "Hail Lucifer! Hail Beelzebub! Hail the King of Babylon!"

The whole world erupted in praise for the monster.

Then Hogwarts called on his aide de camp, Zebulun. His equally hideous lieutenant stepped up. The two small wings on his back buzzed so hard it began to sound like a chainsaw.

"In honor of this day, and in full tribute to our lord and master, I order the massacre of section three!"

Albright froze in fear. That group included his mother-in-law. He knew she had grown up with every convenience in life. This was not good. She had never been mistreated and, for that matter had never mistreated anybody else. This just wasn't fair. People just don't do these sorts of things.

Continuing on with much pomp and fanfare Zebulun said, "So, you think the movie we made happen called the Texas Chainsaw Massacre was frightening, hey? Just watch this."

And with that he began to fly up and down the ranks of the prisoners in section three. Body parts flew everywhere. Heads were lopped off the shoulders of the men and women as they stood there. Helpless. Blood spurted out of their vacant necks as one division of demon angels began to laugh and laugh and laugh.

The prisoners in section two were the prime recipients of the carnage. Brain matter and body parts of every description slammed into them so that, any outside observer would have thought they were included in Zebulun's appalling endeavor.

Albright began to throw up with a violence that reminded him just how sick he had become when he, Big Red and Lizard had hidden behind the bushes to smoke their first cigarettes. His body broke out in a sweat and he began to shake all over. Then, as quickly as the massacre had taken place the strangest thing began to happen.

Right there in front of all of their eyes the separated body parts began to reattach themselves. Heads jumped back onto the same necks from which they had been severed, arms and legs just reconnected themselves and the people became people again. It happened in a flash. In a split second, it seemed. The prisoners were aghast. Stunned silence filled the void left by the screams of the victims who, once again, were standing in their rows with chains on.

"Did you see that?" the man directly alongside Rhodes exclaimed.

"What the blazes is going on?" another shouted.

Just as many others began to curse, cry and scream Hogwarts appeared before them. Behind him stood at least a thousand legions of demon angels. They stood to attention. To his immediate right was Zebulun. On his left another creature even more hideous than the aide de camp. Both front eyes stood on what looked like sticks of granite protruding from his head. Fangs, not unlike the fangs of a leopard, hung out of the sides of the awful gap which was his mouth. In addition, this creature had an extra set of tiny wings attached to his under-belly and the prisoners soon realized why.

Magicullun was the head of wizardry. Lucifer had empow-ered him in a unique way. Not only did he have the authority to cast spells but, more importantly, he was given the responsi-bility to infiltrate every home on earth, and especially children, with books that romanticized magic and wizardry.

"Control their stupid little minds and I will have them in the palm of my hand" the king of Babylon would say.

At the express order of Hogwarts millions of creatures be-gan to appear. Line after line. Rank and file. By the time Hog-warts was ready to speak layers of them hung in rows on top of each other. Albright could not see either the height or the depth of the creatures, there were so many.

"Welcome to eternal hell! You will never escape for all time and eternity. You are the slaves of his royal highness Lucifer Beelzebub the first of Babylon. Whenever he appears in person you will fall down on your faces and worship him."

"We have our instructions. You will be marched from here to your camps. Each prisoner has been allotted and assigned according to the manner with which you served his excellency before you died. But let there be no mistake. You will be in tor-ment day and night forever."

"Once situated you will be trained night and day. You are the mighty army of Satan. When the imposter, Jesus Christ of Nazareth, announces his return to earth, we will be prepared to meet him in battle. According to the decree of Beelzebub, we will join with Gog and Magog. We will link arms with the kings of the north. We will saddle our horses with the false prophet. And we will ride with the one who is our savior and lord, the mighty Satan. That will be the day when all the world will know who god is. Jehovah will be banished and defeated for all time and eternity."

As he spoke the huge iron gates began to rise. What ap-peared to be a bottomless pit opened up in front of the prisoners.

Albright looked back over the right side of his shoulder. He knew where he was and what had happened to him. He had died and was still alive.

He was in hell.

Eight

A t that very same moment he saw himself lying in the casket just below the pulpit of the church he belonged to in New Orleans. There were beautiful flowers all over the place. The church was packed to capacity.

Everybody who was anybody seemed to be there.

He couldn't help noticing the eight governors, including Governor Forester of Louisiana, whom he had helped get re-elected for a second term of office. On the second to front row sat the United States Attorney General Ashton Clarke, the Secretary of State, Robert C. Caldron and many other dignitaries. He'd helped them all, especially when he spearheaded the Republican Campaign in his State. Naturally he had been delighted when the President invited him up to Camp David to do a little trout fishing and play golf with him on the Saturday afternoon just after his weekly radio address was done.

The door leading to the welcome center opened and the pastor of the church appeared and motioned for the congregation to stand up. Albright's entire family appeared at the side door. Nesty had a black dress on, as did his two daughters. Even the grand kids were there. What surprised him were his own siblings.

All five of his brothers were seated on the second and third rows with their families. It was kind of strange to see them in a church. They were always too busy or whatever. Not that Albright was much better. At least he had agreed to allow his name to go forward as a deacon. It was the least he could do. He knew it would be good for his business, especially in the South where such things on a resume were considered essential.

The minister of music, who had usually aggravated Albright because he sang too long and played the music too loud, stood up and made the people sing "Victory in Jesus". Even though Rhodes could just about rattle off the words verbatim, he had never actually sung himself. It just wasn't the "manly" thing to do.

One of his favorite things to do was to go to Louisiana State University's Tiger stadium and watch his beloved "Fighting Tigers" play football. Most people would have agreed that to sit in the Rhodes' box at one of those games was the treat of all treats. He had private parking spaces just under the stadium. The elevator took them straight up to the private room reserved for the big donors of the university. The food was "out of this world". Ralph and Kacoos almost always provided the meal although Albright was known to ship in loads of crawfish from Breaux Bridge when they were in season. The Crawfish Capital of the World could boil those "crawdads" better than anyone between Lake Charles and Pierre Part down near White Castle. What they truly loved were the sausage, corn on the cob and small potatoes that were mixed in with all the Cajun flavors.

It was said that when the golden girls and the marching band came out Albright A. Rhodes would literally come unglued. He loved it. Throughout the game he would "whoop and holler," and anytime the poor referee made a bad call, watch out! Here comes Mister Rhodes. Word was he could sing those songs as well as any person could. He loved to sing.

But not in church! No sir! In fact, people often took one look at Rhodes during the singing of hymns in church and thought he was recovering from hookworm treatment. The difference between Albright's demeanor in church and his demeanor outside the church was very great indeed. He always looked so unhappy when he was in a church service. Now it all seemed too late to do anything about it. Besides, he was watching his own funeral taking place.

There he saw himself. Lying in that casket dressed in his favorite pin stripe suit. The church was packed. His family all crying. And they were singing!

I heard an old, old story, how a Savior came from glory,
How He gave His life on Calvary, to save a wretch like me:
I heard about His groaning, of His precious blood's atoning,
Then I repented of my sins and won the victory.

O victory in Jesus, my Savior forever, He sought me
And he bought me with His redeeming blood;
He loved me ere I knew Him, and all my love is due Him,
He plunged me to victory, beneath the cleansing flood.

Albright began to cry. His heart ached. He wanted to go back and start all over again. Then there were prayers and more songs. The music director began to sing another one of those songs. Before he sang he told of how Horatio Spafford had lost his family at sea. When he returned to the exact spot where they had perished he wrote the words:

When peace like a river, attendeth my way,
When sorrows like sea billows roll;
Whatever my lot, Thou hast taught me to say,
It is well, it is well with my soul.

Albright wanted to go back and make all things well. But he couldn't move. The iron gate was lifting and the abyss was deepening.

The pastor stood up in the pulpit just like Albright had seen him do many times. He said a whole lot of wonderful things about Rhodes and then opened his Bible to John 10:10: "I have come that you may have life and that you may have it more abundantly."

The verse went on to say that Satan comes to steal and destroy. Albright understood exactly just as he did when he first heard all about it at Vacation Bible School in Texas. But now he believed it.

"You're too late you miserable little dipstick!" Albright swung his head around in shock. One of the creatures had read his thoughts and was standing in his face.

"No. Please. You don't understand. I nearly gave my life to Jesus but...."

The creature spat in his face and yelled a horrid stream of abuse. It was so hard and loud that it seemed everything he said went straight down his mouth, through his intestines, down to his toes, and back out of his rectum. He felt like he was having the most vile, violent enema known to man. With that, the creature extended the nails on his fingers. Like a cat bearing down on the wooden leg of a new expensive piece of furniture he ran his nails down the length of Albright's torso. His stomach ripped open and all of its contents spilled out on the ground. A pack of ravenous six legged dog-like animals came and began to eat his entrails despite his protest.

"That'll teach you. Never even so much as think about Jesus! Ever!"

And with that he fluttered away. Next minute Albright looked down and saw his intestines come back together in his stomach. He stood there shaking.

Now he dared not look. But still he saw. And still he heard the preacher.

"If my friend Albright was able to stand here with us, in person, today, I am convinced he would say three things to all of us. First, there is a God. He is the God and Father of our Lord and Savior, Jesus Christ. He alone is the Alpha and the Omega. He is King. He is Lord. He loves every one of us very much indeed. He loves us so much He gave His only begotten Son, the Lord Jesus Christ, to die on a cross for our sin. Second, the only way to God the Father is through the Lord Jesus Christ. His death on the cross provided the only means by which we can be forgiven of our sin. Unless we are forgiven we can never be reconciled to the Father. Not even our money, or our status can give us forgiveness. Only Jesus can do so. Third, Albright would say, "Do it now. Today. Don't wait another second." You see, my friends, once you die that's it. There are no more chances. The Bible says it is appointed to man to die once and after that the judgment."

Albright fought back the tears. He knew it all now. He remembered the wretched old servant by the name of Billy Bob who lived on his property. If only he had listened to his pleas!

The reverend asked for people at Albright's funeral to give their hearts and lives to Jesus. None of his brothers so much as moved.

Next second they closed the lid on his coffin. Some of his family collapsed with grief. They began to lower him into a hole in the ground. Albright felt claustrophobic. He felt as though he was about to choke to death. He wanted to cry out. Break out. They were pouring sand by the spade full on top of him. Big chunks of dirt bounced on the top of his coffin. It sounded like a down pour of heavy rain on a tin roof. Everything was becoming black. The creatures were all around him. He couldn't breathe. But he was still breathing. He couldn't see. But he still could see his family standing there. They were putting roses and flowers and things on the top. The creatures were growling and laughing.

He couldn't get out. Yet he was out!

He was dead. They had buried him. But he was alive.

He was in hell.

Nine

Billy Bob had never seen such a brilliant display of light. He recalled how many times he and the group had gone out to Metairie to stare at Al Copeland's dazzling display of Christmas lights. The fondest memory he had was of the brilliant lights out at City Park. Although he and Sue Ellen had very little in the way of money they always made the best of Christmas. At the park they could stand under the oaks and just watch as car after car drove through the light display.

What he was looking at was beyond description. He lifted his head and tried to explain what he was observing to his wife but she just carried on singing. No one had to tell her which song to sing. She knew it was Billy's all time favorite:

"To God be the glory, great things He has done:
So loved He the world that He gave us His Son:
Who yielded His life in atonement for sin,
And opened the life-gate that all may go in.

Praise the Lord, Praise the Lord, let the earth hear His voice;
Praise the Lord, Praise the Lord, let the people rejoice.
O' come to the Father through Jesus, the Son:
And give Him the glory for the great things He has done."

Billy remembered her favorite saying.
"If you can't beat 'em, Billy, join 'em!"

Well, he thought, here I am trying to get her attention and she's not listening. So, he guessed, "I'll just join her."

So Billy began to sing at the top of his voice. Usually his wife would lovingly touch his hand. Often it would be to get a message to him. Sometimes she would be a little more direct.

"Tone it down a little, Sweetness," she would say softly and tenderly. Especially when they were in church on Elysian Fields Avenue. It took Billy years to accept the fact he could hardly hold a tune in a bucket. But he'd heard the pastor say, on more than one occasion, that what mattered was the heart.

"Make a joyful noise unto the Lord!" he said.

Fine and dandy for him to say but every time Billy felt led to join the sanctuary choir he was turned down flat!

Once again his wife did not seem to hear him singing. There they were in the room behind the rows of trees. Just the two of them. Not one person had been to see him during all his sickness. Excepting Mrs. Rhodes, of course. But then she only came as far as the door. She was scared of the lice or whatever. Since Albright had gotten so sick and had gone to Baptist Hospital there were no more visits at all. Not even to the door. After Mister Albright's funeral they had left for the beach anyway.

It was a sensation like none he had ever experienced. He could see his wife clearly. She kept holding his hand. First one, then the other, then both together. At regular intervals she would stroke his forehead ever so gently. Even at his age Billy had a mop of hair. It was as gray as a naval battleship but she loved it. He loved it too. Especially when she took the front part of his hair and would sweep it backwards to the top part of his head. The she would run those beautiful fingers of hers all the way through over the top part of his head and then down the back to his neck. It would give him goose bumps, especially on his legs.

Tears were coming out of her eyes as she sang. She kept saying, "Thank you, Jesus. Thank you, Jesus!"

He looked around the room and saw something that caught his breath. His Mama was standing there. He was sure it was her. The smile on her face was unmistakable. It seemed like he wanted to reach out and touch her, but he couldn't. She seemed close but was far away. He turned to Sue Ellen.

"Sugar Lump. It's Mama. It's Mama!"

But Sue just kept on singing and thanking Jesus. She reached over Billy and gave him such a precious kiss on the cheek.

The light in the room became even more brilliant. Billy looked up convinced he was looking at the Lord Jesus. Only this time the Savior had taken a seat. He tried to squint his eyes to get a better look. Yes, indeed, it was the Lord Jesus. Just a few moments earlier He had been standing at the right hand of the One who was seated on what looked like a throne. Billy knew He was God.

But now Jesus had taken a seat. He realized there were two people. One on the throne. The other seated next to Him. But it was like they were the same person. Now he knew it for sure. God, the Father and God, the Son. At that instant he became aware of a third person. Right there in the room with him. Billy tried to isolate Him. Perhaps He was in the kitchen or doing something. He looked over at Sue Ellen and saw Him clearly. There He was. Inside her.

Wow, he thought. Wait a minute!

He sat up in the bed again and felt as though he was looking right through his beloved wife. Clear as a bell. Right there in her insides. It was God the Spirit. And then he knew this same person was inside him as well. He looked identical to the two who were on the throne.

Billy had such peace in his heart. He had never been so happy in all his life.

This was remarkable.

Jesus had stood there just a moment earlier and had called to him to "come home!" He had this beautiful smile on His face. He motioned with His hands as He called Billy by name.

Billy responded instantly. "I am coming, my Lord!"

"I have dispatched your escort, Billy. They're on their way!"

Way in the distance Billy Bob saw them coming. There were many of them. They were the most magnificent beings he had ever seen. Jesus had summoned them into His court. Billy could see the Lord Jesus giving the leader a set of instructions. It took a little while and yet it seemed to happen as though time was no longer relevant. The Lord handed the leader a placard with a name clearly emblazoned on it in huge letters.

WILLIAM TERENCE MALKMUS
MY BELOVED SON

The smile on Billy Bob's face was so big and so long it must have resembled the length and breadth of Lake Ponchatrain. He grinned from ear to ear. Sue Ellen even burst into song again and remarked how peaceful and happy he looked.

Billy knew he was dead.

But he had never felt more alive. One more look at his emaciated body revealed the pitiful state of his human remains. Those sores were huge and ugly. His eyes were hollow sockets and his ribs protruded through the skin on his chest. Every human dignity had long left him.

Billy wanted Sue Ellen to see what he could see. Not a sore on his body. Not a mark of any kind. A sweet aroma filled every space. His skin was intact and perfect as that of a new born baby. His missing body parts were whole again. He was perfect!

There they were. He had no problem identifying them. Angels. God's angels. They were coming to get him. The Lord Jesus had dispatched them. Billy knew it. He watched as they harnessed one of the chariots. It was splendidly arrayed. Every part of it was made of pure gold. There were seven angels altogether. Billy remembered how God had created the heavens and the earth and then had rested on the seventh day. The Sabbath Day. This was the Lord's Day. That's why Billy's Mama had always insisted they go to church and honor the Lord Jesus on the Lord's Day. This was God's perfect number. No wonder there were seven angels, Billy thought.

Three of them took up positions on one side of the chariot. Three took up positions on the other. The leader stepped up and stood tall and powerful in the chariot itself. As they began to fly off, millions and millions of angels began to appear. They were singing and praising God.

It brought an incident to Billy's memory he would never forget. It was the time he had managed to acquire a ticket to watch his favorite team play football against the Dallas Cowboys in the Superdome in New Orleans. It happened to be Tom Landry's final game as head coach of America's team.

Even the "nose bleed" section of the dome was better than having to listen to the game on a radio huddled around a fire in the French Quarter. Mister Rhodes' son Rothy had given him the ticket only because all his other options had not materialized. Billy felt like royalty going in there with all those Saints' fans shouting, "Who dat say dey gonna beat dem Saints?" He didn't know too much about the game but he didn't really care. Everyone was so drunk anyway. It really bothered Billy. He even tried to tell a few of the rowdiest ones about Jesus. One of them spat beer all over him and another mocked him and called him a "dirty old religious freak!"

When he arrived back at his room he told Sue Ellen about the long field goal the Saints' kicker put between the posts with no time left on the clock. That meant the Saints had won. The crowd went berserk! Billy said the noise was unbelievable.

But now he heard noise that was anything but noise. It was the most harmonious, beautiful sound he had ever heard. It was thunderously magnificent. It sounded to him like the sound of a million choirs. To top it all they were singing his favorite hymn, "To God be the glory, great things He has done!" Just like his sweet Sue Ellen.

As if this was not enough what Billy saw next transported him to a level of ecstasy unknown to human kind. Surrounding the throne of God were billions of people. They were everywhere. And standing in the front row was his Mama. They were all singing and praising the Lord. Billy felt as though the whole world was watching him.

He turned to tell Sue Ellen but she was on her knees next to his bed talking to the Lord and thanking Him for Billy.

The brilliant light seemed to act like a huge vacuum. It was like it was drawing the angels and the chariot down from heaven. They followed the stream of light as though it was some type of heavenly interstate. The sign with Billy's birth name was now etched across the front of the chariot in a bright red color. Billy understood. His name was written there in the blood of Jesus. That's how it found its way into heaven. Jesus had died for him. Jesus had shed his blood. He gave His life for Billy on the cross. The Bible made it clear that without the shedding of blood none of this could happen. How grateful Billy was he had given his heart and life to the Lord Jesus. His sins had been forgiven because Jesus had shed His blood. Every sin of his had been cast away from the presence of the Lord forever. How grateful he was for a Mama who had never given up on him.

Before he could blink his eyes the glory of God Himself filled the room. The chariot was there. The angels were there. All seven of them. Sue Ellen stayed on her knees. Her eyes were closed. She was singing and praising the Lord.

"I am Michael, first intern to the Archangel Gabriel, chief servant to Almighty God. I stand ready at all times and forever to serve my Lord who is the God and Father of our Lord and Savior, Jesus Christ. To Him be all the praise and honor. He alone is Lord of the heavens and the earth. He is the mighty One. He is creator and by His power He upholds everything that lives and moves and has its being. He is the giver of life. He is omnipotent, being all powerful. He is omnipresent; being everywhere by His Spirit. He is omniscient, being in all and through all. He alone is King. He alone is Lord. He is the Alpha and the Omega. He is the beginning and the end. It is in Him alone that we live and move and have our being. To Him alone we give our praise. So let it be. For as such God has spoken for all time and for all eternity. Amen."

Billy began to praise the Lord.

"William Terrence Malkmus, by the authority vested in me by Almighty God, I have come to transport you into the presence of the King of kings and the Lord of lords."

Ten

A nd with that, the six other angels came and stood on either side of Billy's bed. They reached down simultaneously and began to pick him up out of his bed. Very gently they placed him in the chariot. For months on end Billy had not been able to walk, let alone stand up. The pain had been severe. Now he felt no pain at all. His body had been emaciated. Now it was perfect.

As the chariot began to turn around he took one more look at the woman he loved so much. She had taken his arms and tucked them close to his sides. She then took each hand and with a slight bend in each arm placed the left hand over the right one across the lower part of his abdomen just about where his belly button was placed. Then she walked over to her small cupboard and opened the top drawer. Billy had always wondered what she had in that box all those years. Having opened it she took out the wedding ring he had made for her out of wire the day they had sneaked into the Cathedral to get married. Ever so gently she took Billy's wedding finger and placed the ring on it.

"Thank you, dear Lord Jesus, for giving me such a wonderful husband. Thank you for all the years we spent together. Thank you for saving Billy and for writing his name in your book in heaven. Thank you for taking him home to be with you forever. Please consider coming to get me soon. I know I will see Billy again and will be with you forever in heaven. In the wonderful name of Jesus I pray. Amen."

Then he watched as she took her opened hand and ever so gently ran it down his face across his eyes. They closed.

As he turned his head to watch what the angels were up to, joy flooded his heart. It was like he wanted to be sad for his wife but found it impossible. It was not that he had to fight against inner feelings. He was not suppressing his emotions. There was no sadness in him. All their married life the two of them had spoken about the loneliness of being left behind. As he observed his precious wife he identified the grief in her but found himself elevated to a level of content and joy unsurpassed during his life time. He suddenly had no consideration of time. His age was irrelevant. His existence was now eternal. Immortal. He was dead but was alive forever!

The chariot took off at a speed which defied even the law of gravity. It kind of reminded Billy of the times he would go and sit on the banks of the Mississippi in Kenner, Louisiana right in the flight pattern of those huge planes coming in to land and taking off from the New Orleans International Airport. Of course he had never flown himself. But it amazed him. He was fascinated by the power and speed of those huge things. While holding on to the railing of the golden chariot Billy smiled and thought to himself, "So, this is what it is like!"

He had no idea just how long the trip took. What he did know was that he could see Sue Ellen bend over his body and kiss him one more time on the cheek. Then she stood up and walked out of the door. She brushed past the hedge that hid their little abode from sight, walked across the basketball court and on to the back door of the Rhodes' mansion. One of the Welsh Corgis ran up to her, obviously wanting to play, as usual, but she was a lady on mission. Taking the key she had been given so as to enable her to keep the place presentable and clean while the family was at the beach recovering from their grief, she let herself in. Picking up the huge telephone book she began to browse the yellow pages until she found the number for T. J. McMahon Funeral Home.

Some considerable time later a man arrived in an old black Pontiac Parisienne Station Wagon with a Veterans' Boulevard sticker identifying where it was purchased. Probably ten or fifteen years earlier by the looks of it, thought the grieving widow. Billy observed how curt the man was with Sue Ellen.

"Dis da stiff ya'll called bout?"

He went to the back of his vehicle and pulled a long stretcher out of it. When opened four rusty wheels popped out underneath. He dragged it over to the door of the apartment and went in to the bed where Billy saw him lift his lifeless body out of the bed and unceremoniously dump it on the stretcher.

"That'll be fifty bucks, up front Ma'am," he demanded. "We'll take care of the embalming and even have a couple of cheap coffins. Not more than a hundred."

The pastor of the church arrived and took control of the situation. Sue Ellen had called him and he said he would be right over. The arrival of the preacher caused the undertaker to undergo an amazing transformation in his attitude towards Sue Ellen. He suddenly became polite and most cordial.

Next second Billy Bob saw himself lying in a casket right under the pulpit of the church on Elysian Fields. The door opened and Sue Ellen came out escorted by the pastor's wife, Sybil. All sixteen people in attendance stood up as the pastor began to pray and thank the Lord for the life and testimony of Billy Bob. He opened his bible and began to read from I Corinthians chapter 15.

"But if it has been preached that Christ has been raised from the dead, how can some of you say there is no resurrection from the dead? If there is no resurrection of the dead, then not even Christ has been raised. And if Christ has not been raised, our preaching is useless and so is your faith. More than that, we are then found to be false witnesses about God, for we have testified about God that He raised Christ from the dead. But He did not raise Him if in fact the dead are not raised. For if the dead are not raised, then Christ is not raised either. And if Christ has not been raised, your faith is futile; you are still in your sins."

Billy pumped his arm and shouted at the top of his lungs.

"Yes, Sir! Preach it! Preach the Word! Tell them about Jesus. It's all true. It is absolutely certain. There is life after death. Praise be to God who raised Jesus from the dead. I'm alive forever. Tell them, my brother-in-Christ. Tell them!"

The pastor went on.

"But Christ has indeed been raised from the dead, the first fruits of those who have fallen asleep. For since death came through a man, the resurrection of the dead came also through a man. For as in Adam all die, so in Christ all will be made alive!"

With great compassion in his heart and with a firm conviction about the Bible the pastor told the group about how Billy had come to know the Lord Jesus as his personal Lord and Savior. Although he was dirt poor he was rich. He told many wonderful stories of how Billy and Sue Ellen had shared their faith with others. So many had come to know the Lord Jesus through their testimony.

The whole service was focused on giving praise and thanksgiving to the Lord Jesus Christ. At the end of the message the pastor issued an invitation for anyone in the congregation to give their hearts to Jesus. A young boy, sitting next to his grandmother, stepped out and came down to where the preacher was standing.

"Would you like to give your heart to Jesus, young man?" the pastor inquired.

"Yes Sir!" the boy answered.

And with that the preacher sat down with the boy and led him to Jesus. It was an amazing thing for Billy to watch as he was riding in the golden chariot. The instantaneous moment the kid asked Jesus to forgive him of his sin a thunderous sound erupted across the heavens. The first thing he noticed was the seven angels who comprised his escort. They let go of the chariot and began to fly around in rapid circles making the most awesome sound with their wings. It sounded like a million humming birds all humming at the same time. From their mouths came a torrent of praise and blessing all directed at Almighty God. For a fleeting moment Billy imagined the chariot would go into a tail spin seeing the driver had vacated his responsibility. But to his delight it kept on flying in the same direction at the same speed surrounded by the same brilliant light.

Eleven

Billy Bob's attention was caught by the massing of trillions of angels way up ahead of him. They were all dancing and singing. They looked like they were having a party. Masses of people were standing there hugging one another in every way. Every one was praising God.

Just when Billy Bob was about to turn his attention back to the boy in the church the Angel Michael tapped him on the shoulder and said, "You should have seen the party we all had when you gave your heart and life to Jesus in that prison, Billy!" It was then Billy remembered the teaching of the Bible that the angels in heaven rejoice when a sinner comes to know the Lord Jesus Christ.

They took the body out of the church and down the road to the cemetery where he had buried his Mama. It brought a smile to his face to read what he had written on her tombstone so many years before:

HERE LIES MY MAMA
SHE LOVED JESUS
SHE LIVES WITH HIM FOREVER

While reading the inscription he looked up ahead again to see his Mama standing at the entrance to this huge gate. They were about to land, he guessed. She smiled at him.

Just before the pastor let them lower Billy's body into the grave he turned to the two young boys who were there and said, "Now boys, let me tell you something about this. You see this box here. This casket. It contains the body of old Billy Bob. But he is not in there. That's why we call dead bodies "remains". The moment Billy closed his eyes in death he opened them in the presence of the Lord Jesus. The Apostle Paul said, "to be absent from the body is to be present with the Lord." In fact Billy had not much of a body left when he died. He couldn't even walk, he was so sick. But when he died God sent His angels to come and carry him right into the very presence of the Lord Jesus Christ. Right now, all we are doing is committing dust to dust. You see we were made from dust and to dust we will return. That's why people who reject Jesus have no hope beyond the grave. They are buried and go to hell. Because Jesus died and rose again death has lost its sting. The grave has been conquered. It no longer has a hold on those who belong to Jesus. Billy Bob loved the Lord Jesus and the Lord loved Billy. We know, for certain, that when Billy died, he went straight to heaven forever. And the wonderful thing is that all people who have done the same thing will be in heaven together forever. That's why, even though Sue Ellen has a very sad heart today, she can look forward to seeing Billy again in heaven one day forever!"

And with that they threw sand on his casket and buried it completely in the ground.

Billy smiled. He wasn't in there!

Only a split second had elapsed between the time of Billy's death and the moment the golden chariot touched down outside this massive gate. As his escort took up their positions alongside him Billy gazed in wonderment at the magnificence of the beauty that lay before him. He was marched across a meadow that looked so golden it resembled a massive wheat field ripe for the harvest. A gentle breeze was blowing softly. It was not unlike the kind that blew on a beautiful spring day. Its touch was so soft the wheat stems moved slowly backward and forward giving the impression of the rise and fall of the ocean.

Michael gave a signal and the twelve guardian angels who manned the gate began to open it. There, before his very eyes, stood the Lord Jesus Christ. Michael fell upon his face and cried out "Worthy is the Lamb!"

The whole angelic chorus repeated, "Worthy is the Lamb. Full of grace and full of glory!"

Jesus stepped forward. Billy was so overcome he fell prostrate on the ground and began to praise His very name. The Lord held out His hand and said in a voice that seemed to be heard by no other, and yet was so powerful it echoed across the universe:

"Rise up, my son. Welcome Billy Bob. You are my good and faithful servant. Enter into the joy of the Lord. This is heaven, your eternal home. Come and receive your reward."

A loud booming voice almost disrupted the encounter Billy was having with the Lord Jesus. It came from somewhere over the spectacular river that lay ahead of them.

"My Son, who is that you have with you? Do I know Him?"

"It's O.K. Father! This is Billy Bob. He's with me!"

And with that the heavens rang with praise and worship to the Lamb of God. Billy looked to his left and was amazed at what he observed. It looked like literally millions of people had gathered together. What came to mind was one of those wonderful Billy Graham crusades Billy had seen on television. It had given him so much joy to see hundreds of people coming to know the Lord Jesus Christ as their personal Savior. Only this time those crowds were dwarfed by what he now saw through the gate. There was no way to count their number.

"Who are all these people?" he asked of one of the Angels, who was busy cleaning his trumpet nearby.

"They are the ones whose names are written in the Lamb's Book of Life," he replied. "My name is Anthropos. My Lord charged me with the responsibility of keeping the records of all those names are recorded in the blood of the Lamb. They are the people of God, His children, like you, Billy Bob. Do you see your mother over there? In just a moment you will be allowed to unite. But first we must worship the Lamb."

To his right Billy saw a heavenly host of angels. Millions of them gathered. He was glad of his days in New Orleans because he was able to recognize many of the instruments the angels carried. Needless to say his favorites were the piano, trumpets and trombones. In the background sat one of the angels with a set of drums Billy had never even dreamed about. The band began to play and as they played Billy realized this was no band. It was an orchestra. The sound it produced caused Billy and all the people to fall down on their faces and begin to cry out to God in praise and worship.

Gabriel stepped forward. His face was like the sun and his feet were like two pillars of fire. When he opened his mouth a bolt of brilliant light shot out in a straight line. Billy lifted his head for a second and watched as the bolt of light headed directly across the river and into the far distance. Two angels positioned themselves on either side of the beam of light right on the bank of the river.

"We are the servants of God, Most High. Our names are Alpha and Omega. God gave to us the responsibility of discharging all the duties related to the beginning and the end. As we look back to the great abyss we look toward the beginning. Beyond the abyss lies eternal torment day and night forever and forever for all who worship the Beast. But that is not the beginning. Beyond eternal hell lies the Alpha, who is the One true God who always was because He is from the beginning. We worship Him who is the beginning because He is love from before the foundation of the world. We worship Him because He is the great I am. As we look forward to the great City of God we look toward the end. He is the end which is not because He has no end. He is world without end because He is forever. The kingdom of this world has become the kingdom of our Lord and Christ. He reigns forever.

"To Him alone we give thanks. He is the Almighty who was, is and forever more will be. He has all power and might. All glory and praise and honor are His alone. We worship the King eternal, immortal, indivisible, the only wise God. He is creator and King. Let us all praise His name together."

And with that all who gathered sang the song of Moses, the bond servant of God, and the song of the Lamb, saying:

Great and marvelous are Your works,
O Lord God, the Almighty;
Righteous and true are Your ways,
King of the nations!
Who will not fear, O Lord, and glorify Your name?

For You alone are holy;
For all the nations will come and worship before You,
For Your righteous acts have been revealed.

By now everyone was on their feet. Billy Bob was overcome with emotion to the point at which his heart ached in the presence of Jehovah. What he could not get over was the fact that Moses himself was standing at the head of the masses of people. Billy recognized him immediately and knew who he was. In his hand he held the rod of God, which Billy remembered had at one time been a hissing snake. At his right hand stood Aaron, the one who had served him so faithfully all those years the Israelites wandered around the wilderness.

Then, just as quickly as every one had appeared they disappeared. The beam of light that emanated from the mouth of Gabriel caught them up. They were sucked into it and taken away in the direction of the City of God. Just Billy and the company of those who arrived at the gate the same time he did remained.

A loud cry was heard. Billy Bob thought he was dreaming for just a moment. He cocked his head and there it was again. It was someone's voice. Someone familiar. He looked toward the light and saw nothing but the stream of light. To his right, as far as his eyes could see, was a picture of paradise, its beauty remarkable beyond description. To his left was an equally beautiful scene. All three directions carried no evidence bearing witness to the cry he was hearing. It became more desperate.

"Help me! Help me!"

Twelve

Billy spun around. He knew that voice. He had heard it so many times. It had given speeches on television. It had praised and scolded the children. It had given many an order. It had chastised and rebuked. It had given blessings and cursings. It had called on the name of the Lord on special occasions and had blasphemed His Holy name on others. Yes indeed, Billy knew that voice. It had said many a prayer in church. It had strongly advised preachers on how to run the church and had strongly advised presidents on how to run the country. One word from that mouth had caused the stock market to fall and one word from that mouth had reminded Billy Bob just how inferior he was. That voice had delivered many a graduation speech marked by countless pointers to youngsters on how to make money and live life to the fullest. That same voice had pointed out to his own sons and daughters just how futile and unnecessary it was to "go overboard with religion." There he was.

Albright A. Rhodes in person!

Billy Bob could just make him out. His whole body was engulfed in flames of some kind. He was screaming and pointing at Billy at the same time.

"Billy, it's me! Mister Rhodes. You can call me Albright if you like. I know you. Remember I'm the one who gave you and your sweet, dear wife, that lovely little cottage at the estate to live in. Billy, please....."

But the voice was interrupted.

"Billy Bob, I am the Angel Moriah. I am the servant of Almighty God. He alone is Lord and Master. I worship Him alone. The Arch Angel has commissioned me to escort you to the City of God. The Heavenly Jerusalem. We must leave now. It will be a long and wonderful journey. The trip will take us through the corridors of heaven. Upon arrival you will be met and will be handed over to Ada, one of the Lord's Seraphim. He will take you to the mansion which our God and Savior has prepared for you. Details will be forthcoming."

"But, what about Albright Rhodes? I can see him. He's calling out to me. He seems to be desperate!"

The Angel Michael put a loving hand on his shoulder and said, "We understand, Billy Bob. Do you see the great gulf that lies between us and him?"

Billy turned back again and had no problem seeing what Michael was referring to. Its width was one thing. Billy could clearly see the other side. What was interesting was the other side wall had a gushing waterfall cascading down its walls. The water, strangely, only began some hundred feet down the side of the cliff face so that someone on the other side could see it and hear it but could not reach it without some kind of help. Perhaps a rope or ladder or something would enable persons from the other side to reach down to the water.

The problem lay not in how wide the abyss was in terms of simple mathematics. But it occurred to Billy that even an engineer from the Army Corps of Engineering might not be able to devise a bridge long enough and durable enough to traverse this vast and wide expanse. Having studied this gulf momentarily Billy realized the real problem lay not with the width, but, rather with the depth. He started to walk towards the abyss and the sound of Albright's voice but Moriah checked his intention.

Thirteen

As the gate began to close behind him and the others Billy noticed, for the first time, his outfit had changed completely. He wore a white linen robe that flowed from his neck to his ankles. His footwear looked like those old fashioned sandals he had seen displayed in the shop windows in the Quarter. It made him feel a little bit like a hippie from the sixties but this was so different. Everyone around him was happy. They were all singing hymns of praise and glory to the Lord. Billy loved it. Especially when they began to sing,

Great is thy faithfulness
O God my Father
There is no shadow of turning with thee
Thou changest not, thy compassions they fail not:
As thou hast been, thou forever wilt be!

Great is thy faithfulness, great is thy faithfulness
Morning by morning new mercies I see;
All I have needed thy hand hath provided;
Great is thy faithfulness, Lord unto me!

"The boat is ready to take you to the other side of the Jordan," Moriah announced.

Very quickly the cries and pleas that sounded forth from Albright were lost in the splendor and wonderment of what lay ahead on the other side.

Fourteen

Albright stared ahead with a dead pan expression on his face. He was numb with fear. The creatures were circling in a frenzy. Their facial expressions became intensely more menacing with each passing moment. There was no doubt left in his mind as to the eternal predicament he found himself in. And yet he sensed a determination rising up within his breast. He had to escape. Somehow!

One of the creatures suddenly manifested his presence.

"I am Mara. My name means bitterness. That is who I am. Be assured, prisoners, my job is to make your journey as bitter as possible. My associate, Akton, will give you further instructions."

And with that Akton began to address them all in great detail. He told them the place they found themselves in was known as Gehenna. Albright shifted nervously. It was a horrid sight. What lay before him was a huge ditch. He was not close enough to see how deep or wide it was but he knew it was big whatever dimensions it had. When he squinted his eyes he could see a brilliant light far away beyond the ditch. Every once in a while he thought he detected human movement of some kind. But the creatures kept on disturbing him to the point he could not make full sense out of what he thought he could see. For a second he even thought he recognized one of the people over there but shook it off as silliness. Hallucination was not beyond the realm of possibilities, anyway, considering where he was and all that.

He turned around in a southerly direction and noticed a valley. In the middle of the valley young people were screaming for their lives. Some of the creatures were buzzing around the students taunting them and laughing. Blood and fire came shooting out of their mouths. With their wings they began lopping off the heads of some of them while shouting praise and honor to His Royal Highness Lucifer Beelzebub the first of Babylon. As the youth fell in death and then came alive again, worms, the size of boa constrictors, began rummaging through the piles of stinking garbage that had accumulated. Fire balls popped up constantly and became so intense at one time they found their way over to where the prisoners stood. Many were consumed with fire while others felt their skin burn off their bodies. One man lost his entire facial components, including his nose and ears. But as Akton demanded their attention, his components slowly formed back in place.

The prisoners were now lined up in formation. Each regiment had about twelve hundred prisoners. At the head of each regiment stood a designated demon angel assigned as leader together with about a hundred creatures who hovered above the regiment in a menacing way.

"You will be taken from Gehenna down the three levels that lead to Hades. I promise you nothing but pain, hurt and sorrow for the entire duration of the journey. Upon arrival in Hades you will all be assigned to your camp stations. There you will be trained for the Great Battle. Our forces are devoted to the impending victory of our mighty leader over the upstart Jehovah. As we prepare to march against the one who calls himself the King of Kings our loyalty to Beelzebub will remain supreme. Prepare to descend into Hades!"

Albright's regiment began to march forward in columns of four. Some of the creatures had whips in their hands. The leather tongs had spikes protruding from them so that, with each lash across the back of a prisoner, chunks of flesh would be ripped out and flung about. Flames licked at their ankles. Even Rhodes began to scream in pain. When, finally, they reached the edge of the ditch it became apparent that no person could comprehend either the width, or the depth of the chasm.

Way out in the far distance Albright could now see a beautiful field covered in what looked like wheat. The wind was blowing gently causing the wheat field to look like the rise and fall of the ocean. Standing there in the middle of the field was none other than that old poor fellow who worked on his estate in New Orleans. He looked so happy and peaceful.

Albright realized this man was his only hope. As the flames burned his flesh he screamed:

"Help me! Help me!"

To his amazement Billy Bob stopped and turned around. He can hear me, he thought quietly so as not to arouse the suspicion of the creatures

"Billy, it's me! Mister Rhodes. You can call me Albright if you like. I know you. Remember I'm the one who gave you and your sweet, dear wife, that lovely little cottage on the estate to live in. Billy, please...."

But he never did complete his sentence. First, Billy suddenly turned away and walked in the opposite direction like he either wasn't interested or had been disturbed. Second, one of the creatures came up behind Albright and smacked him so hard in the back he felt all the wind go out of his lungs.

"Don't even think about it, Mister Albright A. Rhodes!"

Mara ordered them to step up to the edge of the precipice. As he peered over the side his stomach churned with fear. It was like peering down the mouth of a massive volcano and reminded Rhodes of the trips his family took to Hawaii.

On one occasion they all flew to the Island of Montserrat in the Caribbean. Using the prime minister's helicopter they circled the gaping wound that had been formed by the massive explosions that had vomited out the innermost parts of the massive mountain. The lava that spewed forth had done enormous damage to hundreds of homes and thousands of acres of vegetation. The British Government was forced to accept responsibility for everything.

Mount Saint Helens also came to Albright's tormented mind. He recalled the time when it seemed the whole of America watched it erupt. He well remembered the old man who had lived near the mountain all his life. The authorities had begged him to leave the area before any harm could come to him. When it blew its lid Harry had no chance of survival because of his stubborn refusal to vacate his home.

This was different, however. This pit was unlike anything he had ever seen. It was too horrible for words. And the stench was so awful the prisoners gagged and heaved with every breath. Huge blobs of hot molten lava kept spewing forth from within its bowels. It seemed as though each eruption was accompanied by a thousand creatures who were flung up and out of the hole, giving the impression of a game of sorts.

The head creature directed them to a stack of ropes and chains piled up against a burned out lump of black molten lava that had seen better days. Their initial orders were to descend to Crypton One which, evidently, represented the first level on the journey to Hades. Four of the strongest men fastened themselves to the stumps of burned out trees which hung precariously over the edge of the chasm. The ropes, which seemed endless in length, were secured around their waists. Albright and the senator made certain their feet were locked in place before the first of the women took hold of the rope and began to rappel down the sheer cliff face of the chasm. One woman froze and began to scream hysterically. Mara gave a signal. Two creatures picked her up and hurled her over the precipice. Her blood curling cries for help were the last her regiment heard of her even though they knew she would continue to live.

Finally Albright took his turn. With his heart in his throat he began to rappel down the cliff face. It seemed to take forever to reach the platform called Crypton One. On the way down he passed ten stations each manned by a number of ugly creatures who shouted the vilest abuse at the prisoners. En route small spots of fire were dropped down his back and into his pants. The worst was when one of these lockets of fire found its way down the front of his pants and into his groin area. Albright could never remember such pain and agony.

Huge snakes and reptiles presented themselves from within the crevices and cracks in the wall of the precipice. At least another three or four of the others could not hold on and plunged out of sight. Finally, and thoroughly exhausted, both Rhodes and the Senator made it to Crypton One.

The prisoners who survived the journey to Crypton One were beyond exhaustion. Their bodies were battered and bruised. All they wanted to do was lie down and rest. Sleep would have been wonderful. But even the thought of it produced an immediate response from Havok who growled and hissed at them.

"You'll never sleep again. Ever! So forget it you bunch of miseries!"

The next stage of the journey into Hades would take them to Crypton Two. Unlike their previous journey they now encountered miles and miles of jungle. There were trees and vines and growth of every kind imaginable. Some thought they were in the Amazon Jungle. Others who had been to South Africa, thought they were on the Wild Coast between the Kei River and Port St. Johns. Wild animals pounced on them. One second a tiger. The next a leopard. The next a ravenous lion. Each visit resulted in a massacre.

The way one lion pounced on one of the young men resembled the kind of scene common to the African bushveld. He waited and then jumped from the top of a rock which protruded from the earth to a height of some thirty feet. His fangs sank into the base of his neck until the artery was severed. Blood began to spew out in jets making the lion even more vicious. The smell of blood attracted many other carnivorous animals. A feeding frenzy resulted producing an orgy of blood none of them had ever imagined possible.

Albright suddenly remembered how irritated he would get when those "hell fire and brimstone" preachers would get on the bandwagon. "Can't stand them," he would tell his family. "All they want is your money! Typical money grabbers!" He particularly hated the manner in which they would say things like, "Be careful of the devil. Be sober. Be in your right mind. The Bible tells us the devil is like a roaring lion prowling around, seeking whom he may devour!"

"Such junk!" he would tell his friends at the club.

"Absolute poppycock! Who are they trying to impress, anyway? Besides, the God I know loves everyone. You tell me. How can a God who is supposed to love everyone send anyone to a devil's hell? Come on! Get serious!"

But now it all seemed to make sense. He wished so badly he had put his pride in his pocket and had listened.

The journey to the camp at Crypton Two was hot and sticky. Even though there was an abundance of vegetation no water was visible anywhere. Many of the trees appeared to have an abundance of fruit. Not one was within reach. Rita Thurston had become so dehydrated she began to eat the leaves of one of the trees. Her mouth broke out in a ghastly chorus of ulcers that festered to the point she could not close her mouth. Even her teeth changed color and began to crumble like a sand castle when hit by an incoming wave on the sea shore.

Mara grinned viciously and reiterated his prohibition on eating or drinking of any kind.

The camp at Crypton Two amounted to nothing. There would be no break, they were told. No rest. It was time to move on to the next level.

Creatures were everywhere. They shouted obscenities and made rude gestures to the prisoners. Mara made another announcement. The regiment stood to attention and was told to put a form of plastic wrapping around their bodies. It resembled Saran Wrap. The kind Nesty would use to keep their sandwiches fresh for the fishing trips in the Gulf. The heat was intense. Then the creatures came by and put one small block of salt in the mouths of each prisoner.

The journey to the third level was excruciating. Water flowed in every direction. The first bridge they crossed took them over a strong flowing river. The water was crystal clear and gurgled as it wound its way down stream. At least one prisoner was so overcome with thirst he threw himself over the bridge and into the torrent. They did not see him again until many years later during the uprising.

Albright could not help notice who the stronger ones were in the group. He began to take mental note of them. He knew they would be needed later on if he and the Senator were ever able to escape.

The final stage of the journey into Hades took the regiment through a series of caves, tunnels and mountainsides. The severity of the climb was cause for great consternation for the prisoners once again. Albright found himself literally dangling in mid air from one cliff face to the next. Many slipped and were not seen again. The survivors rappelled down the final descent only to find themselves in a valley more desolate than the worst Arizona had to offer. This was Crypton Three.

Out of the twelve hundred who had left the outer precincts of Gehenna only some four hundred and fifty had made it through. It would only be after the uprising that the rest would be seen again.

The regiment came to an abrupt halt and gawked at the sight of what lay before them.

"What you see before you is Hades," Mara announced. "You thought you were in hell, didn't you? We'll guess what? You're looking at it. This is the place of the dead."

"Once we pass through the gates you will be assigned to your camp. Consider yourselves fortunate to be included in Beelzebub's army. Until Jehovah announces his so-called big move you will be trained to fight. We will not fail. The imposter will be defeated. His plan is to return to the outskirts of Jerusalem on earth so as to take control. He just doesn't get it. His Majesty, Lucifer Beelzebub, the first, of Babylon, has dominion over all the earth. This Christ has only himself to blame. Our true Lord Beelzebub offered the imposter the opportunity to rule over the earth in exchange for food and something as simple as paying homage to Lucifer. But the fool turned down an opportunity of a lifetime. The cursed Christians are waiting for what they call "the second coming". What fools! In consultation with his royal advisors Beelzebub has chosen this as his finest hour. In a surprise move he will gather all the kings of the earth and march against this pathetic Nazarene. Victory is his. It is guaranteed. In the meanwhile we will prepare for action!"

Albright and company stood and looked ahead in shock. To their immediate front was a huge draw bridge that connected the desolate land upon which they stood with the mainland. At the order of Mara the bridge was lowered in place. The prisoners began to march across to the other side. A quick glimpse over the side rail revealed a bottomless pit that reeked of the worst possible smells imaginable. The Senator began to gag. Others simply vomited all over themselves. It stank like a combination of urine, feces, rotting flesh and every other kind of ghastly odor known to man.

"That, prisoners, is the bottomless pit. You thought Hades was as far beneath the earth as you could go. No, indeed! Hell is just the resting place. What your eyes behold and your noses smell is the place of outer darkness. It is the eternal prison reserved just for miserable people like you. Let it be heard. If any one of you so much as blinks out of line, you will be bound in chains and thrown over the edge of Hades into the bottomless pit. There you will be in outer darkness where there is weeping and wailing and gnashing of teeth. The torment you receive here in Hades pales into insignificance compared to the eternal torment of this bottomless pit. Lucifer has decreed that all who disobey his every command will be bound and cast out. You will do well to heed these words." The entire circumference of Hades was bordered by the pit. There was only one way in and one way out. The bridge. And judging by the guards, not much in the way of cooperation could be expected. Albright made his mental notes.

Hades was worse than anything he had ever imagined. The closest recollection Albright had of anything remotely as awful was the landing on Omaha Beach. He had been one of the lucky ones who made it through the barrage of resistance. Well he remembered the vomiting on the landing craft. Well he remembered the bullets smashing through the bodies of his mates as the huge iron doors were opened. Well he remembered the panic and chaos. But what he remembered most of all was the devastation on that beach-head when the battle was finally over.

Bodies of slain heroes lay in helpless heaps. Trash, steel spikes, barbed wire, blown up vehicles of every kind adorned the beach at every turn. A living hell, he recalled.

But Hades took "living hell" to another dimension altogether. It was simply indescribable. They stood. They looked. They wept. They screamed in agonized response and disbelief.

Very soon the apparent captain of their camp, Malagant, had them assigned. Approximately twenty prisoners were allotted to each camp barracks. Each unit had little inside excepting for the structure itself. They were made of some kind of bamboo and were rat and vermin infested. The floors were pure dirt, full of holes and divots. Within a short time the smell of rotting flesh stung the nostrils of the prisoners as they breathed. Hardly a person was without multiple sores that oozed a foul smelling puss. Although they were exhausted, sleep was prohibited. Malagant barked one order after another in a series of seemingly incoherent instructions that were impossible to follow.

Their days of training had begun. They were in Hades.

Fifteen

Moria offered a hand to Billy Bob as he boarded the boat. The river was beautiful. As they were rowed across the river by two angels the group began to sing praises to the Lord Jesus Christ. Billy was delighted to discover he actually had acquired a beautiful singing voice. He couldn't wait to see Sue Ellen's face, not to mention the choir director at their church.

They soon began to walk directly toward the light. It seemed to shine with greater and greater brilliance the closer they came to the city. They passed over mountains and valleys, through gorges, waterfalls and sights Billy had only ever seen in one of Mister Rhodes' discarded National Geographic magazines. During those days on earth he would often sit in his little hide-away and soak up the pictures of the Napa Valley, Lake Tahoe, and the Grand Canyon and so on. His favorite pictures were the ones of British Columbia in Canada. He often wondered what it must have been like to actually go to places like Lake Louise, Banff and even the beautiful countryside around Jasper.

Now he knew exactly what it must be like! One minute he found himself watching moose grazing quietly like they do on the fields of Kannanaskis, not far from the beautiful town of Cochran, and the next minute he found himself sitting in that quaint little tea-room he had seen in the book that looked down over Lake Louise. Then it was as though he was transported to the panoramic views afforded by the highest peaks of the Colorado Rockies and down to the majestic walled peaks of the Grand Canyon. It was paradise, to say the least!

The group stopped under the shade of willow trees one minute and meandered through forest and vale the next. Every species of animal known to man was seen. It delighted them all when they saw a huge male lion rubbing noses with a lamb. A grizzly bear sidled up to a baby antelope with spots all over its back. The two looked like the best of friends.

Hundreds of deer frolicked in the sun while eagles soared overhead. The streams and rivers were stocked with salmon, trout and bass of every kind. Thousands upon thousands of people moved among the animals. It was as though they were totally unthreatened by one another. Every living creature was in harmony. Billy Bob and his group passed by in wonder and amazement. They wanted to stop and join in but Moriah lovingly reminded them of their prior order of business.

Suddenly it was there. Right in front of them. The Holy City.

"Behold, the City of God," announced Moriah.

"This is the dwelling place of Almighty God; He who is the God and Father of our Lord and Savior, Jesus Christ. This is the Heavenly Jerusalem. This is where our heavenly Father now lives. This is the city which will come down out of heaven from God. It is made ready as a bride adorned for her husband. When Jesus has returned to earth and defeated Satan once and for all, He will rule on earth for a thousand years. During this time Satan will be bound and cast into the bottomless pit. God will command His Angel who has the key to come down from heaven. He will carry a great chain in his hand and will lay hold of the devil who is Lucifer Beelzebub of Babylon."

"At the end of the thousand years Satan will be set free for just a while so as to prove, once and for all, that Jesus Christ is Lord of all. Beelzebub will try to march against Jehovah. They will meet at Armageddon where the evil one will be defeated forever. Together with him will be all those who have refused to accept the saving grace of God in Christ Jesus His Son."

"What happens next?" one of the people inquired.

"The Great White Throne Judgment," Moriah replied without hesitation. "But, I want you all to know we have our information from the same source you have had it. God's holy book. The Bible. The Holy Spirit gave every word in the Bible as God's inspired and infallible word. It is the complete revelation of God concerning all the things we need to know about the Lord Jesus Christ, His Son. God wrote down everything mankind needs to know, not only about the way in which the world began, but the way in which the world will come to an end, as we know it. The pages of this wonderful book also reveal the absolute certainty of life after death. The Bible teaches that after the judgment all those whose names are not found written in the Lamb's Book of life will be cast into the lake of fire forever. Then God will provide for all His children a new heaven and a new earth."

"Wow!" they all exclaimed. "Praise the Lord!"

"But none of us knows of that day or hour. Only God our heavenly Father. He'll let us know in His own time. And when He does, we will all accompany Him back to Jerusalem, where Jesus will set up headquarters."

"Right now let me hand you over to Ada. His job is to take you to your own dwelling place. This mansion was prepared for you the day you gave your heart and life to God by receiving all Jesus did for you when He died on the cross. Jesus reported to God that you had trusted Him as Savior and Lord and so your names were written down in His book immediately."

The Angel Ada fluttered in like a gentle breeze. Unless you were concentrating you would never have known he even had wings. This was a delicate being, soft in texture and extremely soothing in manner of speech.

"Follow me," he said with a gesture not unbecoming to his aura and demeanor.

"Please allow me to provide you with a personal escort through the gates of the City of God. Once inside I am privileged to show you to your personal dwelling place. I think you will love it Billy. When you gave your heart and life to the Lord Jesus in prison I was asked to head up the construction team assigned to prepare a mansion for your arrival here in the City. I was so pleased to hear our King summon Michael and the six others. The construction crew who worked under my direction broke out in spontaneous praise and worship when we saw it was the name of William Terence Malkmus blazoned across the front of the chariot assigned for the trip down to New Orleans."

"Jesus, of course, serves as the Master Architect and interior designer of all the mansions He promised for those who arrive to receive their reward. When He said, "I am going to prepare a place for you so that where I am there you will be also," He meant it. "When we get there you are not going to believe the attention to every detail. So, without much further ado, let's get going, Billy."

Billy Bob tried to take in the magnificence of the City that stretched out before him. It was set high up on a hill. More like a mountain, he thought. Billy had never left the city of New Orleans and so mountains were something new to him.

The only time he felt as though he had climbed a mountain was the day he and Boudreaux had walked over the "high rise" on the new interstate just before Read Boulevard in East New Orleans. So mountains and hills brought out the best delights in Billy. He even felt he had to explain all his "oohs" and "aahs" to some of the others as they traveled from the gate of heaven to this great City.

Both Ada and Billy came to a stop. What they saw was more magnificent than any tongue could describe. The City of God. It shone with the glory of God, and its brilliance was like that of a very precious jewel, like jasper, clear as crystal. The City was surrounded by a very high wall with twelve gates, and with twelve Angels at the gates. One name appeared on the arch way of each of the gates. Billy studied them carefully and then noted they were the names of the twelve tribes of Israel. Judah, Reuben, Gad, Asher, Naphtali, Dan, Simeon, Levi, Issachar, Zebulun, Joseph, and Benjamin. There were three gates on the east side, three on the north, three on the south, and three on the west side of the City. Added to this, the wall of the City of God had twelve foundations, and on them were the names of the Twelve Apostles of the Lamb of God.

Billy couldn't wait to meet them, especially Peter. He wanted to ask him how it felt to have actually walked on water that time on the Sea of Galilee. Billy had tried it once on Ponchatrain and had nearly drowned.

Ada commented on the exact dimensions of the City. Apparently one of the other Angels had been given a golden measuring rod with which to measure the City, its gates and its walls. So, Ada looked pleased with himself when he announced that his report to Billy was "on the button" so to speak.

The City was laid out like a square. It was as long as it was wide. According to the Angel the City was 1,400 miles long, and was as high as its length. The walls were 200 feet thick. The measuring Angel reported the figures in terms of man's measurements. The wall itself was made of jasper, and the City of pure gold. Billy considered it pure as glass. The foundations of the city walls were decorated with every kind of precious stone. The first foundation was jasper, the second sapphire, the third chalcedony, the fourth emerald, the fifth sardonyx, the sixth carnelian, the seventh chrysolite, the eighth beryl, the ninth topaz, the tenth chrysoprase, the eleventh jacinth, and the twelfth amethyst. The reds, yellows, blues, greens, olives, pinks and whites made a dazzling display when seen as a whole.

On one occasion he and Sue Ellen had watched the July fourth fireworks extravaganza on television. It was set up for the entire nation on the mall between the Washington Monument and the White House. Both the president and the first lady were sitting on the balcony of their home watching with the nation in celebration of the Declaration of Independence in 1776. From the humble seat of their tiny little one roomed home at the back of the Rhodes Estate that display of color and light was something neither Billy nor his wife thought they would ever forget.

"She ain't seen nothing yet," Billy muttered to himself with a smile on his face.

"What did you say, Billy?" asked an inquisitive Ada.

"Oh, nothing really," Billy responded. But his smile gave him away.

"Well, Ada, I was just praising our Lord for building a city like this. It is so beautiful. Just look at it. I couldn't help thinking about that sweet wife of mine. Look at her!"

Both Billy and the Angel turned their backs on the City of God and looked out across the fields of wheat, across the Jordan River, over the top of the great chasm, over the top of the abyss and Gehenna and on down to earth. There they clearly observed Sue Ellen sitting on her bed. It was the same bed Billy had been on when the Angels came to carry him to heaven. She was very frail and her age had begun to show since the death of her husband.

She couldn't wait to join her husband in heaven and he couldn't wait to welcome her. But, at least the return of Ernestine and the family from Orange Beach had given her cause to be preoccupied with house cleaning and chores. It really was only late in the evenings when she retired to her room that she had time to think about life after death. One thing she knew was the absolute certainty of life after death. There was no doubt in her mind where she was going when her turn to die arrived.

As he walked under the arch of the one of the gates he noticed the huge letters emblazoned across the overriding section:

WELCOME TO THE CITY OF GOD
THE NEW JERUSALEM

Each of the gates was made of a single giant pearl. And as Billy and Ada stepped onto the City side walk on Main Street it was like stepping onto transparent glass. Only it wasn't glass. It was pure gold.

It made Billy recall some of those fancy shops in the Canal Place shopping mall at the end of Canal Street in the Crescent City. Before security would order Billy and Sue Ellen outside, they would stand at the windows of some of the jewelers and simply analyze the beautiful gold rings, chains and things. He never dreamed that he would walk on gold one day. What a place, this heaven! What a Savior, he thought.

Then, as if Ada could read his mind, the two stood side by side and sang praises to the Lord.

"It's time to meet a few folks I think are anxious to see you," said Ada. "It just so happens one of them is your next door neighbor!"

They had taken a left turn off Main Street and now found themselves in a spectacular suburb. The homes were terrific, to say the least. Everyone was so delighted to see Billy. They waved at him as he went on by.

There it was. Number thirty six Dyson Road. The yard was immaculate. Flowers were everywhere, especially roses. Pinks and yellows had always been his favorites on the estate and once in a while, even Albright A. Rhodes had confessed to some visiting admirer that his gorgeous rose garden existed because of the expertise of his servant, Billy Bob. This place had roses everywhere. And they were all in bloom. Their combined fragrances permeated the air with a freshness unlike any Billy had ever experienced. The front gate had Billy's birth name etched across it in gold letters. Ada hurried to open the gate for his friend as he said,

"Welcome to your heavenly dwelling place, Billy! You will live here forever. Let me show you around and then I will leave you until later when we will all be assembling around the throne of our mighty God!"

They entered by way of the front door. To his left was an immaculate receiving room adorned with a sitting area, vases full of roses and a center tray—for tea, probably, thought Billy. To his right was a room with a grand piano in it. Billy had always loved pianos and had always wished he could play as well as his grandfather. So one can only imagine the smile of surprise when he sat down and began to play like an old professional. Without any difficulty he played "To God Be the Glory" and sang at the top of his voice! He and Ada laughed until they couldn't laugh any more.

Two more immaculate rooms were upstairs. The room on the right had an arrangement of chairs and couches with a magnificent trombone in the center. Billy walked over, picked the instrument up, and began to play "When the Saints Go Marching in" as though he had been playing with Louis Armstrong all his life. The room on the left hand side of the steps was arranged in similar fashion with the exception of one thing. Instead of a trombone there was a trumpet. Billy Bob picked it up and began to play "Amazing Grace How Sweet the Sound, That saved a Wretch like Me!"

Amazing, he thought.

"What's this all about, Ada?" Billy asked. "Come on now. Level with me!"

"No problem, Billy. What we do with our time in heaven revolves around praise and worship. When people come to your dwelling place it is your privilege to lead them in worship. When you visit them it is their responsibility. That's why every home has a variety of musical instruments in them. At times we will all gather around the throne as often as we are summoned to do so by Gabriel. There the Angels are charged with the responsibility of leading in praise and worship. All of you are an integral part of the heavenly choir."

Billy threw his head back and laughed so hard this time. My sweet wife will not need to stroke my hand anymore, he thought.

"All of us are also allotted special assignments in service to our Lord and Master. Among many others these acts of service involve serving directly in the royal palace as well as being sent outside the city gates to carry out duties required by our Heavenly Father. So, we serve and we worship. For all time and eternity. And, oh, by the way, at some time only known to our God, the Lord Jesus Christ will return to the earth to defeat Satan once and for all. We will all accompany Him on the trip to Jerusalem. This will be the time He will establish His 1000 year reign using The City of God as His headquarters. After that the new heaven and the new earth will be spoken into being by Jehovah."

"You mean I am finally going to get to go to Jerusalem?" Billy asked with a high level of anticipation in his voice.

"You got it, Billy," Ada replied. "All of God's children will accompany Him on the return trip. But don't forget the time will come before Jesus' second coming when all believers will be caught up to meet the Lord Jesus in the air. You know. Many of your preachers called this the rapture of the church."

"Remind me when the rapture will take place, please Ada."

"Wish I could, Billy. Beats me. Not even Gabriel knows. A group of us tried to get him to tell us but he genuinely doesn't know. He also told us it was a waste of time even trying to ask the Lord Jesus Christ. Not even the Son knows. Only the

Father. What we do know is according to the Lord's own word. Those who are still alive on earth and remain there will not precede those, like yourself, who have already died. All of you are already here in the presence of the King."

"Here is how it will happen. On command from our Heavenly Father who will be heard loud and clear, trumpets will sound from the heavenly chorus. The Lord Jesus Christ, Himself, will then come down from heaven. Just think about the journey you took from earth to here, Billy. Jesus will leave the palace and will travel out of the gates of the city, over the chasm and the bottomless pit, past Gehenna and then into the eons of timelessness between heaven and earth where the clouds are most prominent. Once in the clouds a most incredible thing will be seen. Every single Christian who is still alive on earth will be caught up to meet Jesus in the air. All the graves, whether they be in the ground or in the sea will give up the dead bodies that are in them. Your human body will be one of them, Billy. This is when your human body will be reattached to the spiritual body you now wear. Of course it will be perfect in every way. The sad part is so many people on earth don't realize the Lord's coming will be like a thief coming in the night.

"Needless to say, knowing the Lord Jesus as personal Savior and Lord results in a win-win situation. Whether dead or alive you are forever in the presence of the Lord Jesus. The wonderful thing is that God loved the world so much He gave His Son to die on the cross. He did not desire for mankind to suffer wrath but to receive salvation through the Lord Jesus. Jesus, in fact, continues to intercede in behalf of man to the Father. The Holy Spirit is actively engaged on earth even as we speak. All of us continue to pray for the salvation of all men."

"One other thing I have to know," Billy asked, "how come there are no beds in this place. And while I'm on that subject there are no bathrooms or toilets either!"

But as the questions came out of his mouth a sudden realization dawned on him. He hadn't taken a bath nor used the bathroom since he had died!

"Billy, Billy," Ada said lovingly. "Perhaps you'll get it any moment. You are in heaven. There is no longer any need for baths and showers and wash basins or even water taps, for that matter. Never again will you be soiled in any way. You will always be spotlessly clean. Inside and out! Never again will you have to use the bathroom. There is no waste matter of any kind. Nothing ever needs to be discarded or thrown away. There is neither junk nor rubbish nor garbage in heaven. And, what's more have you not noticed you have no need to drink anything. Here you will never thirst. As for beds, my construction team decided to leave them out of your dwelling place altogether. They would only be for show anyway seeing there is never any need to rest or sleep in heaven. Here you are in a constant state of eternal rest. Absolute peace is absolute rest."

By now Billy was beginning to get the whole picture. One thing he was glad of was the fine kitchen in his home. He loved to eat even though he knew they would eat nothing that had to die. Death was non-existent in heaven.

He remembered how the Apostle Paul had told the people in Corinth to look to the resurrected Jesus if they wanted to know what happened to a person after he died. Billy remembered his preacher showing them how Jesus ate after He rose from the dead. Of course, what actually happened to the food in His spiritual body was a mystery. Billy now understood as he ate one of the cookies Ada's hospitality team had left for Billy's welcome reception.

There was a knock at the door. Ada suddenly disappeared.

Moving quickly downstairs Billy opened the door and gasped with sheer delight.

"Mama! Mama! It's you! It's really you!"

And with that his mother flung her arms around her son as the two hugged, kissed and were reunited.

"My son. You are here. We are together in heaven with the Lord Jesus. It's just like I told you, Billy. That day you came into my room in New Orleans just before they sent you to jail. Oh, I prayed for you, my son. And for Dwayne. And for Boudreaux. And for all your friends. I cannot tell you the scene here when you gave your heart and life to Jesus in prison. And what about Dwayne! Did the old devil take a beating that day, or what!"

And with that she invited her son to come on over to her dwelling place next door to have tea and sing praises to the

Lord. As he walked through her front door he could smell them right away. The tea table was full of them. Beignets! Just like Café du Monde. And covered in white stuff. His Mama had also prepared a large cup of café ole coffee. What a treat! She reached for her flute and mother and son began to reminisce and sing praises to the Lord.

Sixteen

Albright's barracks backed up to the great divide that separated Hades from the outer reaches of Crypton Three. To his immediate left was the pathway that led directly to the bridge that crossed over the chasm. Multiple creatures guarded both the entrance and the exit points. They were armed to the teeth and on certain occasions horrific looking beasts would pop up from the depths of the bottomless pit to join them. The Senator reported overhearing one of them talk of having been bound in chains and sentenced to 1000 years in the pit for insubordination to Hogwarts. His loyalty was now guaranteed by virtue of the threat to refer him directly to His Majesty Lucifer should he ever be insubordinate again. Such a referral always resulted in eternal banishment from Hades to the place of outer darkness in the lake of fire. Mutiny was not tolerated and was dealt with in the harshest possible way.

Needless to say all the prisoners understood the same eternal banishment would be applied to them should they ever be found disloyal. On just the second day in Hades the prisoners witnessed the harsh reality of this threat when one of the young women complained about the total lack of privacy in the bungalows.

"You want us to show what a lack of privacy is really all about, do you?" one of the creatures replied.

After a quick consultation with Malagant four of the ugly things picked the protesting girl up, marched to the side of the draw bridge, wrapped a huge chain around her writhing body, and summarily threw her over the edge of Hades. Her screams could be heard for a long time. The rest of the regiment was lined up along the precipice and forced to listen to the uncanny screams of what sounded like hundreds of thousands of people who had already been thrown into the pit.

Talk about putting the fear of the devil in me, Rhodes thought.

"It is absolutely certain you served His Highness while you were alive. It is absolutely certain you died. It is absolutely certain you are in eternal Hades. And it is absolutely certain you will serve Lucifer Beelzebub, the first, of Babylon, with undivided loyalty!" Malagant's six eyes darted back and forward and flames shot out of his hideous mouth as he spoke.

"Now, let's begin!"

The regiment was divided into four sections, each comprised of one hundred prisoners. The four sections were further divided into five squadrons totaling twenty in each. The squadrons then divided into units of five each. Of the remaining forty-nine, forty prisoners were appointed sectional, squadron and unit leaders. To his surprise Albright A. Rhodes was appointed Regimental Commander. The Senator from New York was second in command. In total Rhodes had forty eight fledgling warrior leaders and four hundred untrained troops under his command.

Hogwarts, himself, presided over the commissioning parade.

"My council chose you, Commander Rhodes, because of your exceptional leadership during your lifetime. There were many occasions when we thought the imposter Jehovah had manipulated his way into the hearts of your children. His Majesty Lucifer Beelzebub even dispatched a number of us to travel down to your home to help the resistance movement. One example I can cite was the time your grandson came home from that dreaded vacation Bible school at your big church. You will well remember how he was crying. He announced at the dinner table in front of your entire family that he wanted to give his heart to the upstart Nazarene. We were all there but were amazed at your outstanding leadership. In that 'grandfatherly' way you put him on your knee and master minded a plot to distract him.

"First, you told him it was just emotional. Then you 'lovingly' told him he was too young. Then you gave a brilliant speech to the entire family about 'going overboard' and the problems of 'getting carried away' with religion."

"We were cheering."

"But, the best move of all was the way in which you ordered that miserable servant girl of yours by the name of Sue Ellen to go and get the new motorized race car you had bought for his birthday. It never ceased to amaze us how you always had a knack of using your money to buy influence and power. You were great even in the way you would pour money into special religious projects like that rescue mission and that house thing and others so people would be left with the impression you were one of those infernal Christians."

"What truly impressed us was the fact you were surrounded by many other very wealthy people in your church who were committed to the imposter Jehovah. You watched how they gave their so-called tithe to their church as well as major giving to special projects. But you were not impressed. It aggravated you the way they prioritized the imposter's work and their church. It annoyed you, albeit inside your heart, how some of them would come home a day early from vacation just to be in church on Sundays. It made you real mad the way they served in the church and insisted their children and grandchildren follow suit. We loved the way you masqueraded with your riches. You always gave the preacher and other people the impression you were as committed as they were. You sure fooled a lot of people. You always had strings attached and were so good at keeping control of your money. Those of us who were assigned to your life and home were given special recognition when you finally died. Once again Lucifer had won hands down."

"And, thanks to you, it looks like your children and grandchildren have inherited your disdain for following the imposter, excepting when it is politically or socially advantageous to do so."

"Perhaps the best of all were those Sundays you actually went to church. We would stand around and just watch you at work. You would never sing. You always sat near the back so you could get out of the sanctuary as soon as the sermon was over. Remember how you hated that invitation and how you would march your entire family out with you. Your excuse was always the need to get to the club for lunch. We would literally howl with laughter because we knew that was not your reason for leaving early. You just couldn't wait to get out of church. It made you uncomfortable being there in the first place. We also celebrate the way your kids have grown up doing it just like you. But the cherry on the top was the way you criticized the preacher, the sermon, the singing, the choir and just about everything else during your family Sunday lunches at the club. We appreciated it very much because every time you said something negative about the church of the imposter great victories for our Lord Lucifer were recorded."

And with that Hogwarts ordered the entire regiment as well as the creatures to raise their hands in salute of their new commander.

As a mark of personal honor Hogwarts raised the baton of his rank. He pointed it directly at the commander and recited three consecutive "Hail Lucifer's". Two of the creature lieutenants came over and were handed the baton. It was made of steel and had letters attached to the end of it. The two flew to the edge of Hades where they held the rod over the flames that licked up from the lake of fire until the rod was red hot. Then, in full view of the entire regiment, Hogwarts announced their commander would be given the ultimate honor awarded for meritorious service beyond the call of duty.

That was when Albright saw the lettering attached to the end of the iron rod. The number was 666! The lieutenants stood in front of Albright and applied the red hot baton to his forehead. The pain was excruciating as his flesh literally burned and melted above his eyes. No greater honor could, evidently, have been bestowed on one of Beelzebub's servants. The commander was now granted full access to the throne when accompanied by Hogwarts. It was an eternal symbol of gratitude and allegiance.

A briefing followed in an empty barracks.

What amazed the new commander were the explicit details of his job description. His first priority was to ensure the absolute loyalty of his leadership team. The Senator was a lock but he realized work would have to be done on some of the squadron and unit leaders he did not know so well.

Their military training was going to focus on four things: discipline, split second loyalty, tank and armored car training, and guerilla warfare. The latter puzzled Albright. Hogwarts had given much attention to the great battle under Lucifer's leadership. Rhodes understood this would take place at a time in the future precipitated by an announcement by the imposter. He knew the imposter's real name was Almighty God but was not stupid enough to say it. Such foolishness was considered blasphemous by Lucifer and carried an eternal sentence to the bottomless pit.

The final battle, Hogwarts pointed out with much detail, was going to focus on heavy armor. Infantry soldiers were certainly a major factor, as was the air force, but heavy armor remained the key. An amphibious assault was also part of the puzzle. The kings of earth's northern lands, as well as those who had received the mark of the beast on their foreheads, would be included in the fighting force.

But why guerilla warfare? Why all the talk about loyalty to Hogwarts?

Every passing second from then on was devoted to three of the four objectives. Discipline and split second loyalty were considered parallel concepts. The squadrons would march in columns while interchanging positions on the split second orders of their commanders. Their ranks became so precise when they marched it was hard to distinguish any individual who stood out.

Over and over again they marched. Then they ran and crawled on their faces. One minute they were up the next down. Any single trooper who fell out of line or complained was treated in the harshest manner. Some were thrown into the pit, others had various body parts ripped asunder. Several of them were buried upside down in the molten lava beds that had spilt over from within the abyss. Their kicking legs were easily seen as a constant reminder to the regiment. Some were periodically pulled out of their molten graves momentarily. Their bodies were scorched from the upper thighs to the tops of their heads so badly as to conceal any suggestion of human form. Within seconds their bodies would become intact, at which time the creatures would bury them upside down once again for a repeat performance.

And so the agony of eternal torment went on!

The hardest punishment, was the fact that they were not given any water to drink.

Flames shot up constantly out of the ground while dirt lodged in their parched throats. All the while they could hear a steady flow of water. At times it sounded like a waterfall. At other times it sounded like the gentle gurgle of a country brook.

Malagant was particularly unkind. His hideous features accentuated his madness. It was as though he reveled in cruelty, especially when he disemboweled any one of the prisoners. When their parts came back together again he hissed and spat with a mouth wide open to reveal a horrible assortment of angry reptiles. One man was suspended upside down between two poles. Four huge scorpions were vomited out of Malagant's mouth and immediately began to crawl up the face of the unfortunate victim. One scorpion burrowed its way up one of his nostrils, two forced themselves into the corners of his eyes and the remaining one climbed straight into his mouth and down his throat. Each deadly sting was accompanied by a blood curdling scream as the man went into contortions.

Malagant smiled hideously.

The time came when Hogwarts congratulated the commander of the regiment on a job well done.

As a reward the number 666 was branded on the foreheads of the Senator and twenty of the other leaders. The task would be complete, he said, when the entire regiment had been branded.

Unarmed combat, mines and demolition training, the use of hand signals and the study of tactical maneuvers formed the pivotal point of their guerilla training. The amphibious training was undertaken without the presence of water.

In his briefing Commander Rhodes was told to devise a plan based upon a number of tactical maneuvers he had been familiar with during World War Two. The June forty four landings on the beaches of Normandy on D-Day had included 280,000 troops and some 4000 ships. There were five separate beach heads with the Americans landing on Omaha and Utah.

Evidently their supreme commander Lucifer Beelzebub, the first, of Babylon, wanted his regiment to train in similar fashion.

The attack on the imposter Jehovah would be mounted from the Mediterranean Sea in the east and would be joined by ground forces from the north, armored divisions from the south, and guerilla forces from the west.

Albright's troops trained accordingly with one difference. They had no beach head. Instead they had to deal with multiple gasses that caused Hades to constantly tremble and shift with effusive eruptions. Both carbon and sulphur dioxide constantly escaped through multiple cracks and crevices as well as from the edges of Hades. Pulverized lava not only formed itself into uncanny domes of rock but provided an eternal volcanic inferno that periodically opened its disgusting mouth to receive human cargo into its boiling bowels.

On and on it went until Rhodes received his summons to the barracks.

Seventeen

Hogwarts stood with his arms folded. He was accompanied by his chief lieutenants, including Malagant, Mara and the others. They formed the top brass. Malagant stepped forward.

"Regimental Commander, it is my duty to inform you that your loyalty and training have not been in vain. A large group of us have determined to swear our loyalty to our supreme commander, Hogwarts, the first, of Euphrates. We have grown tired of the dictates of Lucifer. You have trained your regiment well. Together with thousands of like minded regiments stationed in Hades we will march against Lucifer and defeat him. All hail Hogwarts!"

And with that he and Albright stepped outside just in time to witness the gathering of scores and scores of prisoners numbering in the millions. At the head of each regiment stood a commander and surrounding each battalion flew thousands of shrieking creatures.

The way had been prepared for mutiny.

Malagant stepped forward and presented Vulcan to them as supreme commander of the Order of Hogwarts.

"I am Vulcan, appointed supreme commander of the Order of Hogwarts, the first, of Euphrates. We swear our allegiance to Hogwarts and will march together to defeat Beelzebub. All hail Hogwarts. Hail Hogwarts!"

The troops all raised their fists in the air. Thousands, if not millions, of creatures began to fly around in frenzied circles.

Fire came from their mouths and reptiles of every kind darted in and out of their hideous mouths in an exceptionally morbid anthem of twisted praise and adulation. Hogwarts came out of hiding and acknowledged the thunderous cheers of all who bowed before him.

"May all who hear me on this day know that we will defeat Lucifer and his gang of demons. We are greater than these. I alone am appointed to defeat the imposter. I alone am capable. We are ready and prepared to march on to victory. Every one who marches with me will forever be spared the bottomless pit and the lake of fire. You will have one more six added to your foreheads in honor of your allegiance to me. Because of your service and devotion you will spend the rest of eternity in Hades. Only Beelzebub and his cohorts will be banished to outer darkness where there will be wailing and gnashing of teeth forever. Vulcan will now give you my orders."

The supreme commander of the Order of Hogwarts outlined the battle plan. Albright could not believe what he was hearing. For the first time he learned there were thousands of layers of Hades just like the one he was stationed in. Each layer was called a trough and contained multiple camps identical in construction. Beelzebub's castle stood alone on the extreme left hand side of Hades on the other side of the abyss on level with Crypton three. Access could only be attained by crossing the bridge because not even the creatures could pass over the abyss without being sucked into its horrible fire.

In order to guarantee their quick and undetected crossing, the draw bridge guards had also sworn allegiance to Hogwarts on the promise of promotion. This made it possible for the army of Hogwarts to cross over to Crypton three.

The Senator looked Albright squarely between the eyes. Many conversations had taken place about the possibility of escape. They knew it was a hopeless endeavor unless they could cross over the bridge.

Both men well recalled what they had seen from Gehenna. Billy Bob was on the other side. They had seen him clearly. Albright realized the old servant was his best hope if he was to escape. They had begun a conversation. That Billy had heard and seen him was beyond question. Something had interrupted the conversation.

From time to time during their battle preparations both Rhodes and the Senator had glimpses of that beautiful place but never long enough to establish anything concrete. They could even see people in the distance, but, again, never the way in which he had seen and identified Billy Bob.

Mara interrupted their planning session.

"New recruits coming in," he said.

The regimental commander looked toward the draw bridge and noticed a whole group of new prisoners being hustled across the bridge. They looked awful. Suddenly one young man in the group broke away and ran towards Rhodes.

"Bebo, it's you Bebo!" Albright's seventeen year old grandson cried out.

He was the oldest of the grand children and the first to call Albright by his grandfather's name. The term of endearment stuck when Ally tried to pronounce his grandfather's name as a baby. They clung to each other for a second weeping from deep within their souls.

"Ally, my boy, what are you doing here?" He asked with tears streaming down his anguished face. "You are too young to be in this place!"

"Last week end Daddy took me down to the camp at Grand Isle for a special father and son time just before graduation. You know, Bebo, how we used to go there all the time to catch Reds and go out into the Gulf on the family boat, especially on Sundays."

Ally's grandfather winced. No one needed to remind him he was the one who had taught his family to make the best use of Sundays for recreational purposes. Even though he was a deacon in their church, loyalty to the House of God was never a priority for him. He had sown the seeds of eternal destruction for his entire family.

The boy continued. "We left out of Venice because the boat had been in for a new coat of paint. Daddy wanted us to get out to the reef where we always caught a ton of Reds. As you know, Bebo, that's about fifty miles out into the Gulf. A tropical depression had formed somewhere out near Cancun and moved in our direction overnight. It was unlike Daddy not to check but the outer extremes hit us hard. A huge wave swamped the boat and I went over the side while trying to trim the sail. I ended up drowning Bebo! It was horrible. I could see myself in the water. A bunch of the ugliest looking creatures came and got me. They put me in this wagon and chained me to the floor. All the while I watched in horror as a huge shark came up and ate most of my body. They still haven't found my head or any of the other parts. I watched the whole thing."

"What about your Daddy, son?" Rhodes dared to ask.

"A Coast Guard chopper found him drifting about a hundred nautical miles south east of Corpus Christie, Texas. He and Mama are grief stricken. Bebo, I watched my own funeral at our church. I've never seen so many people. But, Bebo, we have got to warn them. None of the family have any interest. And none of them take seriously the absolute certainty of life after death. What can we do Bebo?"

Very quickly Rhodes shared his plan with his grandson. Together with the Senator they would cross the bridge along with the other regiments. In the middle of the ensuing battle against Lucifer they would escape and retrace their steps through the Crypton levels back to Gehenna. From there it would be easy to follow Billy Bob's instructions and cross over to where he was living.

Only Albright's position as commander prevented the creatures from hauling Ally off. Hogwarts, himself, had made it clear that his servant had to be trusted by the creatures. They dared not contradict his orders.

Vulcan gave the order to move out. The draw bridge was lowered into place. Troops began to march across the great divide. Ally stuck close to his grand father.

Eighteen

Billy loved the social life in the City of God. It consisted of continuous fellowship with his Mama and neighbors. Singing remained his favorite occupation especially when they sang songs like "Gimme that old time religion," and "I'll fly away" and "When the roll is called up yonder I'll be there!"

Shortly after one of these visits Ada stopped by Billy's dwelling place to see how he was getting along. He also had good news. A new arrival had made it to the City of God. So Billy and his Mama made the journey to an adjoining neighborhood. He begged Ada to tell him who it was but the Angel just gave him one of those delightful, almost mischievous, looks.

There he was, in the front yard of his dwelling place. None other than Dwayne. The two men looked at one another for just a split second before running in to one another's arms. Billy was overwhelmed with joy as the two men and his Mama sang praises to the Lord Jesus Christ. Needless to say every missing detail of their lives, from the time they left the prison in New Orleans until their passing into the presence of the Lord, was shared. Both men could not wait for their respective wives to join them.

The subject of marriage came up. With total contentment in their hearts they understood how it was in the Heavenly Jerusalem. Marriage was no longer an issue.

Just like the Angels had never been given in marriage, so it was they would not be married in the City of God. Each person had their own individual dwelling place. Jesus had promised this when He said, "I am going to prepare a place for you!" Spouses and loved ones would live next door, so to speak.

Both Billy and Dwayne engaged Ada in a lengthy conversation about the subject because it had been so very important to them while they were alive on earth. But now it was different. Their bodies had been changed, anyway. They no longer had any need to be emotionally, physically, or sexually fulfilled because they were perfect in every way. Besides this, there was no need to reproduce and replenish anymore. Billy also reminded Dwayne that no one in heaven had any desire to possess or own anyone else. And they certainly would never pledge any kind of covenant or allegiance to any but the Heavenly Father. There was no need to even think about a covenant in which two people promise to love, honor and cherish in sickness or in health, whether rich or poor, or for better or worse...! There were no such things!

Dwayne, Billy and his mother all smiled and laughed with such joy. Dwayne even told of one of his neighbors who had been married more than once on earth. When his first wife had died of cancer he thought he would never marry again. But years later he met a wonderful Christian lady who had found herself in similar circumstances. Now all three of them were in the City of God living close by one another and not the slightest bit concerned about which one of the ladies were rightfully married to the man. They neither talked about it nor so much as thought about it. There was no need.

An unexpected visitor showed up at Billy Bob's front door. It was Michael, the deputy to Gabriel.

"Hadn't seen you in a while," Billy stated with a smile of love on his face.

"Been real busy about the Father's business," Michael answered. "Lots to do when you serve the King of kings and Lord of lords. I just returned from a tour of duty down on earth. Our Master continually dispatches trillions of us to move around the earth watching out for the children of God. I have been sent to supervise the operation so many times but this one was the best of all. I was assigned to the small children detail. Our Savior has a very special place in His heart for little children. He constantly reminds us that heaven is likened to them particularly in regard to their innocence and purity. He truly gets upset when some parents intervene in their children's lives and do everything they can to prevent them from coming to know Him as their own Lord and Savior. We've even heard horrific stories about parents actually telling their kids they are too young."

"Do they really think God is incapable of knowing when they have reached their age of accountability?"

"He knows when they come to an understanding that their sin separates them from our holy and righteous God. So He always dispatches us to go on down there and do all kinds of things to protect them from coming to harm and danger. Of course there are those children who suffer from fatal diseases and even those who are killed at an early age. Those are the hard ones to deal with because their parents find it difficult to understand why God would allow some children to be protected and others not. And, to make it even worse, some begin to question their own faith when it seems like the Lord has not answered their prayers. But, now that you are in heaven, Billy, you can see this is not the case. You now have complete understanding. God's ways are not man's ways, are they Billy?"

Billy was fascinated.

"But this is not the reason I am here today, Billy. The words I have shared with you are trustworthy and true. But, the Lord, the God of the spirits of the prophets, has sent me to show you things that must soon take place."

Billy was moved to the very core of his being. He fell on his face at the feet of Michael and almost started to worship him. Michael stopped him in his tracks.

"No, Billy! Do not do it! I am a fellow servant with you and all who belong to the Lord Jesus Christ. We worship only Our Heavenly Father who is the God and Father of our Lord and Savior Jesus Christ. Come, Billy. I have been asked to bring you before our Father."

And so Billy walked out of his home and began to follow the Angel on a wonderful journey down Main Street in the City of God. As they walked they were joined by hundreds and then thousands and thousands of others. Billy's Mama, Dwayne, they were all there. It was like a mighty chorus of song and praise. A marching band headed the procession with Angels playing every kind of instrument known to man. Billy loved "When the saints go marching in," and sang with great gusto the part that had changed a little to, "Oh Lord I am among that number," instead of "I want to be among that number."

The great street, of course, was of pure gold, like transparent glass. This was the moment he had been waiting for with much anticipation. As they reached the center of the city Michael stopped them and made a speech.

"Fellow servants of the God Most High. As we enter the holy of all holies it is my duty to remind you there is no temple in the City of God. There is no need."

He was right, Billy thought as he looked around. All he could see was a light so brilliant he could neither describe nor comprehend it.

"The City does not need the sun or the moon to shine on it. The glory of the God gives it light, and the Lamb is its lamp. In fact, the nations of the earth will walk by its light, and the kings of the earth will bring their splendor into it. On no day will its gates ever be shut, for, as you already know, there is no night here. The glory and honor of all nations will be brought into it. Nothing impure will ever enter it, nor will anyone who does what is deceitful or shameful ever be granted permission to enter the City of God. Only those, like yourselves, whose names have been written in the Lamb's Book of Life, are brought into the presence of the King of kings forever."

A great silence fell upon the entire gathering.

It was not a stunned silence. Nor an awkward silence. Rather it was a kind of wonderment silence. They were all awestruck as they gazed upon the scene that began to unfold before their very eyes. Every saint of God stood as though paralyzed in praise and worship.

Michael had much more to say. He pointed out the river of water which represented life. It was clear as crystal, and flowed from the throne of God and the Lamb. It flowed down the middle of Main Street in the heart of the City. On each side of the river stood a beautiful tree. Michael reminded the group of the significance of the trees. They were the trees of life. Each bore twelve crops of fruit. He explained how the leaves were symbols for the salvation of the people of the earth, representing the intercession of the Lord Jesus Christ in behalf of the nations of the world.

Not that the group needed any reminders, but Michael did point out the total and complete elimination of the curse of death from the City of God.

This was the spot. It was right there. The center piece of all that mattered. The throne of God! In the heart of the City. The center of the universe. The center of all creation. Here the servants of God would serve the King forever. Here they would see His face.

It had to have been the most magnificent sight Billy had ever seen. And surrounding the throne appeared to be concentric circles of spectacular mansions, all adorned in splendid glory.

Michael pointed to them as he continued his detailed explanation.

"The dwelling places on the outer circle are those of the great prophets and servants of the Lord. They have their reward. The distance of your dwelling place from the throne of God is in direct proportion to the rewards you received at the judgment seat of God. The dwelling places you see in the outer circle surrounding the throne represent the crowns of glory awarded by our Father for faithfulness in ministry and service to the King. As such it will not be any surprise to you when I tell you that Noah, Moses, Abraham, Elijah, Isaiah, Jeremiah, Daniel and so many other people who were great in faith occupy the homes closest to the throne of God. Numbered among these will be many to come as well as mothers, fathers, sons and daughters who served the Lord Jesus with all their heart, soul and mind."

Billy certainly had no problem with that arrangement.

So many people, many of whom were hardly known on earth, had worshiped the Lamb with unparalleled devotion. Countless others had given their lives and had become martyrs for the faith over the centuries. Many had been persecuted for the righteousness of God. One of those living there was the little old widow Jesus had talked about who gave all she had to

Him. He called it "the widow's mite," if Billy remembered correctly.

"What about that row of houses on the inner circle?" someone in the crowd of worshipers asked.

"Oh, those. They are the mansions which were prepared for the Twelve Apostles. Perhaps after our visit to the throne of God we might be able to stop by and visit with some of them, if the Lord has not sent them on an errand."

There it was before them arrayed in splendid glory. The throne of Almighty God.

As Billy looked around it appeared that millions of people had come together. Angels were flying here and there singing songs of praise and adoration. Every inhabitant and every creature fell prostrate before the one who sat on the throne.

The sound was like the roar of a mighty rushing wind.

To Billy Bob it reminded him of a massive combination between a number of sounds he had become familiar with when he lived on earth. One was the roar of the Nascar speedsters as they careened past the checkered flag on the final lap of the Indianapolis 500. Billy loved to watch Nascar on television and had always wished he could go to one of the races. His favorites were Bobby Unser and Jeff Gordon. He would have been happy to go to Darlington or Bristol in Tennessee, or even the Daytona 500. Mister Rhodes always went with all his family and a lot of friends. He paid for everything and everyone. But he never asked Billy Bob. So he would just watch it on television when it wasn't on cable. He and Sue Ellen could never afford cable.

The other sound was a little different from the roar of stock cars. Billy often sat on the banks of the Mississippi River and watched the river boats, packed with tourists, going by. He would be so lost in his thoughts sometimes that the initial screeching sound made by the calliope on the Natchez would make him jump out of his skin. It was intense and shrill to the ears. The steam would gush out the pipes of the calliope as the river boat pulled away from the dock. Billy loved to sit there and watch while holding hands with his wife.

But this sound went way beyond anything. Every single person and every single angel joined the chorus.

"Hallelujah!
Salvation and glory and power belong to our God,
for true and just are His judgments.
He has condemned the great prostitute
who corrupted the earth by her adulteries.
He will avenge on her the blood of His servants.
Hallelujah!
The smoke from her will go up for ever and ever!

Surrounding the throne were twenty-four elders and four mighty angels. Together they fell down on their faces and began to worship Almighty God who was seated on His throne.

At that very moment, Jesus Christ, the Son, stood up from His seat at the right hand of the Father.

"Let the whole of creation praise the Father. Praise our God all of you who are His servants. Let everyone who fears and respects Almighty God, praise Him, whether small or great. Praise Him no matter how many crowns of reward you received at the judgment seat of God!"

Billy looked upon the face of the One who had met him at the gate of the City and had welcomed him into God's presence. His face shone with the radiance of the glory of God. Billy looked at the Father who was seated on the throne alongside and to the left of the Son.

They were separate but equal. They were distinct but exactly the same. They were one.

When Billy gazed in awe upon the Son he was looking in the face of God. When he shifted his focus to the Father he realized he was looking at the Son. It was like he was looking at only one who was seated upon the throne, and yet he could distinguish two.

And that was not all there was to it.

As he peered into the loveliest face he had ever seen he saw a third person. He knew who this was because he had seen the same one in Sue Ellen as he passed away from the earth. The Holy Spirit. Yes, they were three in one!

As they praised the Father a conversation began to unfold. The Father turned to the Son.

"My beloved Son, I am well pleased with you. You obeyed me all the way to your death upon the cross. I thank you for your willing sacrifice in behalf of my creation. Because of you, all people can now come into my presence and have fellowship with me. My ultimate purpose in creating man was to have fellowship with him. It was such a sad day when Adam and Eve chose to sin against me in the Garden of Eden. From that moment onwards sin reigned upon the earth. The devil, that old serpent who is Satan, has had a field day with my creation. But because of my love and grace and mercy, you, my Son, went and allowed man to take your life so that all who believe in you can now have direct access to me. It was a great moment when I raised you from the dead. The look on Beelzebub's face was unbelievable. He really thought he had you dead and buried. But you triumphed over death and the grave. You are life. Now all who have the Son of God in their hearts have eternal life. Thank you, my beloved Son! Please be seated at my right hand because you alone continue to intercede in behalf of all people. It is my will that all people be saved for all time and eternity. I do not want any single person to perish without knowing me. That is why I constantly used the word "whosoever" in my complete revelation."

And having spoken to the Son, God turned to all of his servants who were gathered before His throne.

"Because of the sacrifice of my beloved Son, your Lord and Savior Jesus Christ, I have adopted every one of you as my sons and daughters."

Billy looked around. Everyone beamed from ear to ear.

"You have received eternal life. The moment you repented of your sin, confessed them to the Lord Jesus and believed in your heart that I had raised Him from the dead, you were saved for all time and eternity. You are now my elect. I made this plan to save you and all people from before the foundation of the world. Any single person who goes to an eternal separation from me in eternal hell, goes there, not because I have sent them there, but because they have chosen to go there. Every one who calls upon the name of the Lord Jesus Christ will be saved."

A holy silence surrounded the throne as God continued to speak.

"What is more, my beloved Son asked me to send the Holy Spirit down to earth to take care of these matters after Jesus ascended back into heaven. The Son and I call Him the Spirit of Truth. You know Him as the Holy Spirit. He is me. We, together, are one in the same person. We are the Godhead. The triune God. While it is true we are one person, we each have our own responsibilities and functions to perform. Now I know the world has had a problem receiving the Spirit of Truth because they neither see Him nor do they know Him. But not in your case, my sons and daughters. You know Him because He lives within you."

Billy immediately thought of Sue Ellen. God went on.

"When I brought Jesus back to heaven to be with me His work was finished. There was nothing more He could do to earn the salvation of all men. The problem was all the people I had created that were left behind on the earth. Just one look at the twelve disciples made me realize how desperate you all would be without a leader. So, I sent my Spirit. In so doing I was, in effect, sending you myself. I knew there would come a day when you would realize that Jesus is in me and I in Him."

"So, Jesus had to come back to be with me in order for my Holy Spirit to go down to the earth and do His work. That's exactly what He has been doing. It is His responsibility to convict the world of sin, of my righteousness and of the coming judgment. In regard to sin, His conviction is critical because the world does not believe in me. In regard to righteousness, because without the Lord Jesus in person the world no longer had the means to see me. And in regard to judgment, the Spirit's power and presence was absolutely necessary because Satan is the prince of the world. He is the father of lies. He is deceiving people by telling them I do not exist and that I could never possibly send anyone to what he would call a "devil's hell". The Spirit of Truth guides all people to me because I, alone, am truth. And one thing is for certain. My Holy Spirit never speaks for Himself or draws attention to Himself. He always directs everything to me. He only speaks what He hears from me. As such He brings glory to me."

With that loud peals of thunder ricocheted across the heavens. The great multitude gathered began to shout praises to the Father. It sounded like the roar of rushing waters and the booming claps of clouds set on a collision course.

"Hallelujah!
For our Lord God Almighty reigns.
Let us rejoice and be glad
and give Him glory!
The wedding supper of the Lamb is coming,
and His Bride has made herself ready.
Fine linen, bright and clean, will be given for her to wear
Because of the righteous acts of all the saints."

They looked and saw written across the seat of the throne: "King of kings and Lord of lords."

It was at that same moment Billy noticed something new. Every person who stood in the presence of the Lord had the name of Jesus Christ written on their foreheads. Their faces glowed with light. Everyone realized why there was no longer any need for the light of a lamp or the light of the sun. The Lord God had given them light. They were in His presence. They would reign with Him forever.

Nineteen

Hogwart's orders had been meticulously carried out by Commander Rhodes and every battalion. The troops were ready for battle. Beelzebub's days were numbered!

Endless ranks of troops marched in squadrons across the bridge. None dared even so much as to take a fleeting glimpse over the edge. Views of the bottomless pit were neither sought after nor desired. Too many prisoners had brought back tales of unmitigated terror and torment.

The lake of fire, which burned endlessly throughout the length and breadth of the pit, took its pound of flesh in continuous motion. The never-ending free fall through its fiery orbits was not unlike the re-entry of the NASA space shuttles that literally burned up as they raced perilously through the outer reaches of space and the inner pull of earth's gravity. Even the creatures themselves shook in abject terror as they recounted their visits to outer darkness. Even the light caused by the eternal fire was swallowed up into bland oblivion by the endless nothingness of its sheer bottomlessness.

The battle plan was simple but brilliant. Each regiment was given special instructions by Vulcan, the supreme commander of the Royal Order of Hogwarts. Creatures who had switched sides in the hopes of higher rank and other promised favors, had provided detailed information concerning the layout of Lucifer's castle.

Set high up on a mountain, Beelzebub's throne provided a lofty perch from which to orchestrate the affairs of his vast earthly domain and Hades. The castle resembled a gothic cathedral surrounded by three massive towers that provided concrete support to three gateways. Each gate had the numbers 666 emblazoned across their top posts, while the main gate had a huge inscription in gold lettering.

THE CITY OF SATAN
HIS ROYAL HIGHNESS
LUCIFER BEELZEBUB I
OF BABYLON

In addition each of the three gates was specifically named. The first was named The Beast Gate. The second was named The Dragon Gate. The third was named The False Prophet Gate. On top of each of the three gates sat an evil spirit in the form of a hugely grotesque and gigantic frog.

Out of the mouth of each frog came multitudes of evil spirits in the forms of demons. As they were spewed out of their mouths the demon spirits were dispatched to journey up to earth to sow havoc on lands, nations and people. Their primary responsibility was to act as the special envoys of Lucifer. Some infiltrated human minds, others wreaked havoc by causing wars, others served to distract people who were being drawn into the heart of God by the Holy Spirit, others mastered the art of subtle persuasion, suggestion and innuendo just to carry out the will of their evil master.

Their ultimate mission was to begin the work of the final battle against the imposter.

They were to go out to the kings and rulers of the whole world and gather them for the battle on the great day to be announced by the imposter Jehovah.

Only Lucifer's top creatures resided within the walls of the city of Satan. No human prisoners were permitted to enter into the city unless requested to do so, and then, only when accompanied by a creature of high standing, like Hogwarts.

With 1000 regiments forming a battalion, Vulcan ordered four battalions to approach the Beast Gate, four the Dragon Gate, and four the False Prophet Gate.

But Vulcan was a master tactician. He had worked for Lucifer for a long time and was very familiar with some of his likes and dislikes. Hogwarts was now his new master. And he had some very interesting bits of information that would provide critical information to his new lord. What he reported provided the ideal opportunity for Hogwarts to make his move against Lucifer.

Beelzebub was not at home. He was out of town on business.

Vulcan went on to explain there were certain times and special occasions when Beelzebub took matters into his own hands, so to speak. In other words, Vulcan assured Hogwarts, Lucifer did not send representatives or emissaries, but handled matters personally.

The festivity held each March in the City of New Orleans, was one of those times. Mardi Gras!

Every year he paid a personal visit to the Crescent City. There were others for sure. He was known to make personal trips up to earth for heavy metal rock concerts, the holocaust in Germany, the time when Saddam Hussein murdered his own people with deadly gas, the civil war in Serbia and other places around the globe, times when books were being written on witches and wizardry (especially when children were targeted), and so many other times when the dark side of life was being highlighted.

And, even though Vulcan almost felt a little stupid saying the obvious, Beelzebub loved getting involved in the means he used to attain his ends. Things like drugs, alcohol, satanic cults, and others, like using bad company to bring young people down to his horrid level of evil.

What he particularly enjoyed was the subtlety with which he would sneak up on unsuspecting people. He was like a hissing snake. He hated morality of any kind and loved it when people marched for the right to do whatever they wanted to do regardless. They called it freedom of expression or speech but Lucifer knew better.

They were serving him. He loved that.

He loved the way people began to murder unborn babies by the millions in the name of choice. In America, for example, he had persuaded a lot of people that the most important issue in life was politics, not spiritual belief. He licked his chops when senators and other influential people touted morality over spirituality. He sure didn't want them to realize that what God had to say about life was more important than any political correctness or manifesto.

So, he often became involved personally. This was one of those times, according to Vulcan.

Lucifer Beelzebub, the first, of Babylon, had departed with an entourage for New Orleans to help accentuate the meaning of "Fat Tuesday." What better way to bring down a people than to throw caution to the wind.

His timely absence provided a magnificent opportunity for the mutineers. They positioned themselves outside the walls of the castle and waited for the order to attack. Heavy armor had been drawn into position and an assortment of tanks, numbered by the hundreds, was carefully concealed in hull-down position.

While all the details of the pending insurrection were talking place, Albright had met with his second-in-command with great frequency. Their plan of escape was simple. When the attack began they would move to the rear guard. This tactic had been successfully shared with Malagant. It made much of the advantage afforded the regimental commander. From the rear he would be able to direct a more precise bombardment on the castle. Ally had been assigned to the senator as his aide-de-camp.

Vulcan stood tall and proud as he gave the order to attack.

All hell broke loose. It seemed as though an atomic bomb had been unleashed on the castle.

Albright, the senator, and Ally began to run. As they ran something astounding happened. It was a voice. A familiar voice. One they had heard the day they arrived at the gates of hell.

"You fools. You imbeciles. You sorry sons of treachery. You insolent dogs. Do you not know who I am? I am Lucifer Beelzebub, the first, of Babylon. I am who I am because I am. I am immortal. I am invincible. I am your worst nightmare. Only the imposter has any remote hold over me. That is why I will defeat him once and for all on that day. That is why you are here. That is why I am the father of lies. That is why I have dominion over the earth."

"Did you really think I was not here? I am here but I am also there. I am everywhere. I do not need to leave my throne to carry out my will. My throne is everywhere. It is in the hearts of millions of people who are exceedingly wicked. That's where I am. I rule in the hearts of mankind. He does my bidding. He carries out my every command."

"Seize Hogwarts! Seize Vulcan! Seize Malagant! Seize the traitors! I will make an example of them so all will know I am the great I am!"

To the utter astonishment of the prisoners, not a single bomb had so much as touched the city of Satan. The frogs had been busy. Every explosive device thrown at Lucifer's fortress had been caught and swallowed up by his ghastly body guards. The meal was fitting. His domain was impenetrable!

Hogwarts and his lieutenants were paraded in front of Beast Gate. Beelzebub stood on the head of the frog. With fire gushing forth from his mouth he pronounced sentence.

"For your treachery you will be taken in chains and hurled into the bottomless pit. There you will encounter outer darkness where there is wailing and gnashing of teeth. You will be tormented in the lake of fire forever. You are eternally damned. Never again will you look on my face. Never again will you walk the streets of Hades. You are hereby denied the privilege of returning with me and my legions to the earth on that great day. This will be the day when I, Lucifer Beelzebub, the first, of Babylon, will defeat the imposter once and for all. This will be the day when I will be crowned king of kings and lord of lords. I alone will be the lord of the heavens just as I am now the lord of all the earth. For thus I have spoken. Thus it is said. Thus it will be done!"

And with that Hogwarts and his band of traitors were summarily hurled over the edge of the abyss. Their screams and cries for mercy became one with the multimillion voices that comprised a horrible chorus of agony that already reverberated up and out of the pit of endless nothingness.

Twenty

G abriel stood before the throne of God.
"Our Heavenly Father has asked me to inform all his servants concerning upcoming events. There is much to do and Satan will be cast from His presence forever. We worship the King of kings and the Lord of lords! He alone is worthy!"

The multitudes cried, "Holy, holy, is our Lord God Almighty!"

"At a time known only to the Father, the Lord Jesus Christ will return in the clouds to receive all who are alive and remain until His coming. They will be snatched up from the earth to meet our Savior in the clouds. What will follow on the earth will be a seven year tribulation. The anti-christ, who is already preparing himself, will rise to the seat of power and prominence among those who are left behind. At his side will be the dragon and the false prophet. They will assist him in casting the great delusion upon the people. For three and a half years there will be a false peace on earth. Even the children of Israel will be drawn into this scheme."

Billy and his Mama held hands.

"After three and one-half years has passed by the great tribulation will break out on the earth. This will be the time when God will grant permission for four angels to put the seal of God on the foreheads of those who come to trust in Him during the tribulation. They will be massacred and martyred for the sake of the Lamb and will be blessed. They will have washed their robes and made them white in the blood of the Lamb. Never again will they hunger or thirst. The sun will not beat upon them, nor any scorching heat. The Lamb at the center of the throne will be their shepherd. He will lead them to springs of living water and God will wipe away every tear from their eyes."

One of the people standing near to Billy asked about the promised return of the Son of God to the earth.

"It will be during this time that we will all wait for the announcement. Jesus Christ will return to the earth for the second time. Heaven will open and the Lamb will be mounted on a white horse. His eyes will be like blazing fire and on His head will be many crowns. He will be dressed in a robe dipped in His own blood and His name will be the Word of God. We will all follow Him as the armies of heaven, riding on white horses and dressed in fine linen, white and clean."

"What about us?" another asked. "Do we need to get ready to fight a battle or something against Satan?"

Gabriel held up his hand in a gesture indicating the need for silence.

"The beast will gather the kings of the earth to come against our God and defeat Him. However, out of His mouth will come a sharp sword which will defeat Satan and his cohorts once and for all. The beast and the false prophet will be captured and cast into the lake of fire and brimstone. The angel of God will bind him up and throw him in the abyss for a thousand years while our Savior rules from Jerusalem. We will surround His throne. After the thousand years God will sit on the great white throne. All whose names are not found written in the Lamb's Book of Life will be cast from His presence into the lake of fire. This will be the moment when the New Jerusalem, which we now live in together, will come down out of heaven to earth. This will be the time when our God will create the new heaven and the new earth. Earth will go back the its pre-Garden of Eden days when all was completely perfect. You will all live forever back on the earth and will walk the same pathways you walked during your life time. Only, this time, it will be unblemished by sin, death and darkness. The heavens will be completely accessible and will form the eternal reaches of the glory of our God and Father."

The multitudes praised the Lord in the beauty of His holiness.

Jesus stood to His feet once again.

"Behold, I am coming soon! My reward is with me and I will give to everyone according to what he has done. I am the Alpha and the Omega, the First and the Last, the Beginning and the End.

"Blessed are those who wash their robes, that they may have the right to the tree of life and may go through the gates of the city. Outside are the dogs, those who practice magic arts, the sexually immoral, the murderers, the idolaters and everyone who loves and practices falsehood.

"I, Jesus, have sent my angel to give you testimony for the churches. I am the Root and Offspring of David, and the bright Morning Star!"

And then the Lord Jesus Christ reminded all within the sound of His voice as to the meaning of His sacrifice on the cross. He stood and pronounced the true meaning of His grace and mercy. He reiterated the fact that all people, regardless of sin, could come to Him when they recognized their own sinfulness and confessed it to Him alone.

Billy knew this was Jesus' final assurance to the world that He had no desire for any single person to be cast away from His presence.

With a radiant smile on His loving face God the Son continued.

"Come! Whoever is thirsty, let him come; and whoever wishes, let him take of the free gift of the water of life!"

Oh, how much Billy wished in his heart that all people who had not yet died would hear the voice of God. Billy felt like Jesus said this to settle, once and for all, man's debate about some being elect and others not. That's why He gave man the Great Commission to "go into all the world!" That's why the very name of Jesus is an invitation for all people to come to know Him.

Gabriel then made an announcement. All servants in heaven would be given special assignments in preparation for the great day. The council of Angels had coupled them together according to the allotment of crowns. Those, like the prophets and martyrs, who had been given many crowns, were coupled with those who had fewer crowns. The purpose was not for anything but fellowship. The Angels knew how desperately some of them wanted to spend time with some of the great heroes of the faith.

So, one could only imagine the sheer joy in Billy Bob's heart when Abraham was assigned to work with him.

He well remembered the time he was hanging around the restaurant Sue Ellen's mother worked in. It was quite by accident that he sneaked in to the men's restroom at the exact same time a very famous movie star was in there. Everybody in America knew this man. In fact, there were more security personnel in the restaurant than other people. He was in New Orleans to film his new movie which went on to win all kinds of awards.

But that encounter paled into insignificance compared to meeting Abraham and then actually going to work with him. Only being in the presence of the Lord Jesus could rival this!

Their assignment was to go outside the city gates and tend to the vineyards that grew up and down the banks of the Jordan River. They were interspersed with beautiful fields of wheat. Billy remembered passing through there on his way to the City of God.

Twenty One

With the pitiful screams of Hogwarts and his cohorts ringing in their ears, Albright, together with the senator and his grandson Ally, ran like never before. They passed the abandoned draw bridge at Crypton Three and began the arduous journey back up towards Gehenna.

Each cryptonic level presented fresh challenges. Rhodes was grateful to have Ally with him. His young arms provided much needed strength especially when climbing some of the sheer cliffs and traversing some of the mountain ledges. On more than one occasion a group of new recruits would pass them by.

Fortunately for Rhodes's small group of fugitives word about the failed uprising had already reached the creatures who were escorting the new prisoners. Besides this announcement, Lucifer's personal welcome at the gate of hell was now accompanied by every explicit detail of the botched mutiny.

The result was they dared not depart from their express orders to deliver the prisoners to Hades. The newly appointed supreme commander of the order of Lucifer, Zoarts, saw to it personally.

So it was, the unlikely trio passed by each convoy in relative security.

Disaster struck only one time when they found themselves climbing the sheer rock face up to Gehenna. Ally was, understandably, petrified. He'd always been bothered by heights. No one in the family would doubt how frightened he was.

On one of the family trips abroad, his father had talked him into para gliding. The whole family was there, staying at the majestic Victoria Hotel in downtown Interlaken, Switzerland. Ally would spend hours watching the para gliders landing on the mall in front of the hotel. Together with his father and several cousins, they had driven in a van up one of the mountains having signed up with a set of instructors. Ally never forgot the sheer terror in his heart as together with his instructor, he leaped off a mountain overlooking Interlaken at some 3000 feet. Once airborne he settled down and rather enjoyed the panoramic ride down to the grassy landing strip.

But heights were never his favorite thing.

This escape route was different. Sure!

With flames continually licking at his feet, Ally hesitated on the final ascent to the summit. It was a fatal move. As he looked down his stomach went into hysteria. His grip loosened causing him to fall some 5,000 foot to a ledge below. Both legs were shattered, his pelvis broke into splinters and his neck bone snapped like a twig. As he writhed in pain, observed by a desperate grand father, his body reassembled enabling him to suffer the terror of climbing to the summit one more time. He fell weeping into his grand father's arms.

By some miracle they made it to the top, all the way back to where this terrible nightmare of a journey had begun. The gates of hell! Gehenna!

Gehenna was just as horrid as before. Albright did not want to waste time. He had to relocate Billy Bob.

In surveying his surroundings, he quickly found what he was looking for. Behind him lay the awful picture of Gehenna. In the far distance he could see the gates of hell. Beyond that Rhodes could clearly see the earth.

It was a strange feeling. Even the senator remarked about it. He felt as though he was looking up from within the bowels of the earth. It was like he was inside the earth's stomach. The picture he had of New Orleans was from the bottom up. It looked three dimensional in a strange sort of way.

Ally began weeping beside him. They could see Ernestine sitting in her favorite chair in the den. Sue Ellen was serving her a cup of her favorite English Breakfast tea. Albright could even see his five brothers, including the one that lived in Ruston and the other that lived in Lake Charles. All five had done well in business.

It was obviously Sunday morning because Rhodes could see his church full of people. Both he and Ally began to weep uncontrollably.

"We've got to get word to them, Ally. If we don't, they will all end up coming into this place of torment," Rhodes pleaded.

"But Bebo, you were the one who always stopped us from giving our lives to Christ. All of us loved you so much and we thought if you said something it was right. You always loaded us down with material things and told us the most important things in life were to be socially accepted, politically well connected and have lots of money. You said money was what made the world turn, remember!"

Bebo wept.

The three men did their best to survey the land before them. To the east and west there was more Gehenna. Flames popped up everywhere and hot, volcanic lava kept oozing through the cracks in the crusted ground.

What interested Albright, in particular, was all he observed before him. The massive pit that descended into Hades was triangular. The point at which all the new prisoners had begun their descent and where the three of them had reemerged, was at the mid point of the lower line of the triangle.

A signpost he had not noticed initially was implanted in the molten lava to his left. Closer inspection revealed a map. Each of the three points of the triangle was named for the "Unholy Trinity." The Beast, the False Prophet and the Dragon. The three levels of crypton were clearly outlined as was Hades and the city of Satan within its precincts.

What really fascinated Albright was the notation that headed the map.

THE GREAT DIVIDE

This designation stood above the top point of the triangle. As such it lay directly ahead of where they were standing.

All three men noticed they could skirt the edges of the pit leading down to Hades and the abyss. It was like a massive triangular hole in the ground surrounded by Gehenna on the immediate outside and bordered by the gates of hell on the upper sides and the Great Divide on the lower side. The lower side pointed in the direction of heaven, the upper in the direction of the underside of the earth.

In truth it was the Great Divide that caught the undivided attention of Albright.

There he could see some things. First, there was a foggy mist that rose up from the Great Divide. None of them could make sense of it but they knew they had to get there if there was any hope of escape. Beyond the mist Albright could see the brilliant light he had seen the first time he had passed that way. It began somewhat diminished but intensified in brilliance until it became a single flash of light similar to that of a very bright star.

They followed the pathway, first to their right and the point of the triangle called the False Prophet. Taking a sharp left at the turn they began the difficult process of maneuvering over and around the spurts of fire. The continual trembles and shifts caused by the effusive eruptions never ceased to announce an impending volcanic eruption of massive proportions. Gasses blew up and out of the cracks and crevices like petrified air sacks desperately trying to escape eternal confinement.

Every volcanologist and geophysicist Rhodes had ever known warned of the devastating effects of the sulphur and carbon dioxide gasses on human lung tissue. These were so intense it was as though they were engaged in a relentless pursuit of trying to please Pele, the Hawaiian goddess of the volcano.

As they rounded the False Prophet all three stopped dead in their tracks.

Twenty Two

———————

Beyond the rising mist was the most serene and beautiful scene they had ever laid their eyes on. A cursory glance left the impression of a gentle breeze blowing softly across a massive field of golden wheat. The brilliant light which shone out from way ahead gave the wheat a decided "waves of the ocean" look. In the middle of the wheat field was a vineyard. The leaves were as green as the grass Albright had seen so often as a member of the elite Augusta National Golf Club. The only things missing, he thought, were the azaleas on "Amen" corner. But the colors were there. It was magnificent.

The men were speechless.

Bunches of grapes, ripe, luscious and delicious, no doubt, hung there as if to accentuate the torment of the already tormented and desperate threesome. Rows upon rows of them dangled in the warmth of the golden light.

Even Albright could remember the sermon his pastor had preached that mother's day. The family always went to church on mother's day. It was one of those obvious exceptions for greater good, if not just plain respect. During the last Mother's Day service he attended just before his death, the pastor reminded the congregation of the words Jesus had spoken to His disciples, describing the way He would love and nurture them and all of His children.

"I am the true vine, and my Father is the gardener. He cuts of every branch in me that bears no fruit, while every branch that does bear fruit He prunes so that it will be even more fruit-ful. You are already clean because of the word I have spoken to you. Remain in me, and I will remain in you. No branch can bear fruit by itself; it must remain in the vine. Neither can you bear fruit unless you remain in me."

Rhodes remembered Jesus going on to say, "I am the vine; you are the branches. If a man remains in me and I in him, he will bear much fruit; apart from me you can do nothing. If any-one does not remain in me, he is like a branch that is thrown away and withers; such branches are picked up, thrown into the fire and burned."

He winced. Those words stung him to the core of his being now. He could see the vine and the branches. It all made sense, the vine, the branches, the fruit.

Then he saw them. And now he realized he had seen them before.

Twenty Three

Two men stood side by side. They were busy talking and picking grapes. They seemed so happy. They looked so clean. Almost perfect, thought Rhodes as he watched them from his vantage point.

Then he recognized both men.

"Abraham! Abraham! Father Abraham! Sir! Over here! It's me! Albright."

He had no doubt it was Abraham. Although he had never met him personally, he certainly enjoyed all those great stories about him at Vacation Bible School. So much so he recalled how he, his five brothers and sister had all put on a play about Abraham and Isaac for the family gathering when they were children. The story he loved, in particular, was how Abraham obeyed God and took his only son up the mountain side to offer him as a sacrifice. The brothers had even offered to practice sacrificing on their sister but their mother had gotten wind of it when she saw one of the brothers sneaking out of the house with a carving knife and a box of matches. Her instincts led her to follow him where she found sister already tied up and laid out across a broken down wall on the farm.

He loved the way his Sunday School teachers would use illustrated story books to show Abraham loaded down with donkeys, servants and so on as he approached a hill side. He told his servants to wait there while he and Isaac went to sacrifice to God and then return. He loved the part about tying Isaac up and nearly stabbing him to death but for the provision of a ram that was caught up in a bush nearby.

Only now, Albright thought, the story wasn't just a nice fable someone invented to give preachers something to say in the pulpit.

In fact it was all about the way God provided His Son, the Lord Jesus Christ, as the only sacrifice acceptable to Him as the necessary means by which the sin of man could be forgiven.

Albright began to weep again. He wanted to convert to Christianity now.

But it was too late!

He believed now. But it was too late! He knew there was only one more chance. Abraham had to help him. He had a direct line to God. He could go through Abraham. After all, he was a priest, or a bishop or something high up in the church. Surely God would listen to him and have mercy on his soul.

"Abraham! Abraham!" He shouted and shouted. "I'm over here with my grandson, Ally. Same name as me. Albright. I know how much you loved your boy! Abraham, over here! Who's that with you? Isaac? No! It's Billy Bob! Abraham. Sir! I know him. I know Billy! Just ask him. He'll vouch for me! I'm the one who provided him and his lovely wife, Sue Ellen, that beautiful cozy little cottage in the back of my estate in New Orleans. At no cost to them either! Abraham, Abraham! Please you've got to listen to me. I need your help. My life depends on it. I am tormented in this flame!"

The threesome stood on the edge of the Great Divide. They looked pitiful. The senator and Ally had been burned so badly their bodies looked like charred remains.

Neither could speak.

Albright was not much better off. But at least his eyes were intact and his voice was still there.

Abraham and Billy stood on the other side. The looks on their faces reflected resigned compassion. There was no malice or anger or grief or anything for that matter. Their faces were recognizable but somehow different. A kind of glow was evident. Kind of like an angel look, Rhodes surmised. And what a contrast to the creatures!

Everything about them, in fact, was different. Their surroundings, their demeanor, their kind faces. Albright knew what it was and he knew, without a shadow of a doubt, where they were. In heaven! It made him more desperate than ever. This might be his final opportunity. He'd blown it while on the earth. He'd been too busy, too skeptical, too disinterested—so now he was having to deal with the consequences. Big time. He was a man's man! Accept the facts, he thought.

But he also knew God had to be reasonable. He had grace and mercy as two of His primary attributes. He was just! Besides, many a preacher had said with great gusto, "God does not want anyone to perish." Good time for God to deliver, he concluded in his mind. He really wanted to prove those preachers right, all of a sudden.

That's when "the light came on." He was, after all, a Louisiana boy! The religious culture was all around him. How could he have been so stupid? So blind! They all believed in purgatory! This was it!

It had been a while since he had felt so hopeful. There it was. There he was. Silly fool, he thought in chastisement of his own short sightedness. He remembered how important it had been for some of his closest friends to have a priest administer last rites just moments before the onset of death. It all made sense now. The closer to death your sins are forgiven, the shorter your time in purgatory! And was Hades purgatory, or what? And that is why Lucifer always seemed to put a time limit on those he sentenced to the bottomless pit. With the exception of Hogwarts and company, that is. But mutiny was obviously in another league. Made sense. The bottomless pit was just a further illustration of the system of purgatory. Obviously mass murderers like Charles Manson and Henry Wayne Lucas and Hitler and Stalin and so forth deserved to go deeper into purgatory than Hades. That's why he had never even been in jeopardy of being thrown into the pit. In fact, he had even been selected as a regimental commander. Now he understood why he had been able to escape with relative ease.

Yup, he congratulated himself. After sentence had been carried out and the penalty paid in full, all people would ultimately be elevated out of hell and into heaven. Heaven was everyone's destiny. Some just took a little longer to get there and that was fine as far as Albright was concerned.

So Albright found himself trying to peer over the edge of the Great Divide. Clouds of mist rose up from somewhere below. He realized it was a waterfall not unlike Niagara Falls in New York. This was only thousand times bigger. It seemed to stretch out forever.

The three of them were so thirsty. They could see the water. They certainly could hear its mighty roar. But they could not touch it.

Great relief washed over the complexion of his deeply anxious face. He now knew their predicament was going to be resolved. And the reason Ally was with him, among the obvious, was his youth. He had been a good boy. A model grandson, polite, respectful to his elders, a hard worker and morally sound in his judgment. No long term in purgatory for him, Bebo agreed. He sighed with a sense of relief. No hard feelings, as far as he was concerned. He'd been at it longer anyway. Same for Ernestine. She'd never cheated on him or anything remotely like that. So she would, in all likelihood, pay only a very brief visit to this god-forsaken place. But not Guidrot!

"That sorry son of a sea-faring catfish," he yelled out. "Wife beater, whoremonger, money grabber. The insolent little puppy!" Was he in for a surprise, or what? Probably will spend many years cuddled up with those demon creatures, Albright figured out with a smile of satisfaction on his charred face.

Abraham and Billy went on about their business. Pangs of thirst came over Albright again. His tongue was so swollen it felt like a chunk of wood in his mouth. The sound of water was about to drive him insane and, besides, Ally and the senator looked bad, real bad!

"Abraham!" he shouted while cupping both hands around his mouth in an effort to accentuate the sound.

"Father Abraham! Sir! Please listen. This is very important. I can see you and Billy are busy picking grapes. But if you don't help me...there are creatures here...this place is horrible...we are being burned alive!"

He knew Abraham was the man to talk to. Not Billy. He had been a Chief Executive Officer most of his life. Besides, if there was one thing Mister Rothschild had taught him it was to honor the man at the top.

"It's only the big dog's bark that produces the bite, my boy," he would lecture from time to time. Another of his favorite sayings was "Never tell a pet gorilla where to sit!"

Rhodes had become both the "big dog" and the "pet gorilla." Nothing aggravated him more than one of his executives going to the wrong "dog" to get something done.

"You want it done right," he would teach his staff, "go to the big dog. Otherwise you are wasting your time and my money!"

With renewed confidence he appealed to Abraham's stature as a great leader, deliverer of nations, mighty warrior, and elder statesmen.

"Sir! General Abraham! Sir! One small request, please Sir! Won't you send Billy Bob over to our side? You see we are dying of thirst. I can hear water gushing down there somewhere. I know it's down there. Over the edge. But I have no means to reach it. I can also see that gorgeous stream running beside you and through the vineyard. Perhaps, Sir, if I could ask you one favor. Could you instruct Billy Bob to simply get a cup of water and bring it to me to cool my tongue? I am tormented in this flame."

This was such a change for Albright. He had so much money during his lifetime he probably could have bought all the coke machines in Louisiana. He didn't know what it meant to be thirsty. Ever! And the choices. Cokes, Sprite, root beer, Seven-Up, tea, coffee, water, sweet, unsweet, diet this and that, fruit juice...the list goes on. It was unbelievable thinking about it while pleading with Abraham.

Now all he wanted was one little drop! Just one cup, perhaps, to cool his tongue!

But his request was denied.

Abraham looked up from his activity.

"I see you and hear you, Mister Rhodes. Listen to what I have to say to you. Remember that during your lifetime you had everything your heart desired. You were a blessed man and yet you refused to give your heart and life to the Lord Jesus Christ. Billy Bob, on the other hand, suffered greatly during his life time. But, nonetheless, he gave his life to the Lord Jesus. Now your circumstances have been reversed. Billy is now perfectly complete forever whereas you are perfectly incomplete forever. The difference is in the choices you made for or against Almighty God. You see, Albright, you cannot serve both God and Beelzebub at the same time. You cannot sit on the fence. You are either for God or against Him."

All of a sudden it dawned on Albright. He was dead but still alive. That much was absolutely certain. More than that it was absolutely certain the life he was now living after his death had not cancelled his ability to remember. His mind still worked. What Abraham had just told him was an undeniable fact. He knew it. What's more he had the capacity to remember all he had done and not done while he was still alive on earth.

So much for those who believed in everything from reincarnation to the obliteration of the human soul after death. Once you're dead, you're dead! That's it, they believed.

"Live today because tomorrow you are going to die!" was the basic underlying theme of Mardi Gras. That's why "Fat" Tuesday was always followed by "Ash" Wednesday.

Abraham was not through with Rhodes. He had another bombshell to drop on him.

"Besides all this," he continued with compassionate authority, "there is a Great Divide between us. You and I can see it clearly. It's called a chasm. It is as eternally long as it is eternally deep. God, our heavenly Father, made it that way. The side we are on is called heaven. The side you are on is called hell. This is where our God, the Father of our Lord and Savior Jesus Christ, lives in the New Jerusalem, the City of God. Where you are is hell. It is the place where Satan lives. You know him as Lucifer of Babylon. It has within its borders, not only Hades, but the bottomless pit. That will be the place where Almighty God will cast Lucifer and all his cohorts to burn in the lake of fire forever."

Albright began to plead.

"But Abraham, you must understand that..."

Abraham kept on without paying any attention to the man's urgent interruption.

"You chose to go there, Albright. You were given many opportunities, many reminders, many wake-up calls and many invitations to accept Jesus as your Lord and Savior. They ranged from church revival services to the plane wreck that nearly took your life to friends who begged you to turn your life over to Jesus. Remember how you promised God that if He spared your life after your wreck you would serve Him for the rest of your life. Well, Albright, you were spared because God had a plan for you. You could have been such a blessing to the Kingdom of God with your leadership and riches. Yet, within a month you had forgotten your part of the bargain and had gone about your life as though God was only someone to pull out of a paper bag and dust off every now and then when it suited you."

Rhodes winced in fear and trepidation.

"The problem, though, is even if I wanted to send Billy Bob over to you he couldn't get there. And if, by some means, you wanted to come over here, you couldn't either. You see, Mister Rhodes, heaven and hell are two irreconcilable differences. They can never come together. They are fixed for all time and eternity. This is an absolute certainty."

Albright sank to the ground in despair. His mind was spinning. He had always been able to exert his influence on other people. The swaying of minds was something he prided himself on. Millions of dollars had often been at stake. He had been a shrewd and calculated manipulator of minds. Despite insurmountable odds against him, his power of persuasiveness had usually won the day. No one could touch his ability to rationalize. Many a board room was witness to his uncanny logic. Even the media had decried the remotest probability of some of the corporate mergers he had brought about. Too much money, they would claim in their articles. Regulations too embedded in the law, they would argue. Too much risk, they would agree!

This time he began to have feelings somewhat reminiscent of being check-mated by one of his grandchildren. He found himself cornered. There was no room to move. A quiet conviction was carried across the chasm in the voice of Abraham. There was something firm and definitive in what he was hearing. It was like the auctioneer's hammer had been slammed onto the table for the final time. The verdict was about to be announced. Sentence was about to be passed. Albright knew it!

His emotional juices began to take a turn in a different direction. The eager hopefulness he arrived with had changed to passionate negotiation. Anger found its root deep within his breast and bore testimony to the giant of a man he had been during his lifetime. Does he realize who he is dealing with, the chairman of Texas Mete pondered? His anger was quickly laid aside for fear of alienating this mighty warrior who may well represent his only chance for survival and rescue. Besides Ally was there. Leave me, then, but take the boy he thought for but a second of true paternalistic heroism. It all changed in one instant. This is not a dream, he thought. No, Sir! This is true. He knew it. The hammer had fallen. Sentence had been passed. A life sentence!

Albright A. Rhodes sank to his knees in despair.

This was the end of the road. His mind began to race. He retraced the steps of his lifetime. He thought of his growing up years and the reverend that no longer looked stupid and foolish; the grand estate in the Garden District of New Orleans; his wife and children; the grandbabies; his five brothers; his sister. They were still on earth. He could see them. Panic began to rear its ugly head. The sound of his sobs echoed across every millimeter of the great divide. His hands at first hung limp by his side as though paralyzed by the deadly bite of a baboon spider. Then, in a state of infantile quandary, he slouched over his knees with his back drawn down in parallel limbo. The picture portrayed the pathetic heap of a once high and mighty man with his back broken. His chest heaved in a futile effort to suck the last vestiges of air out of the molten lava upon which he lay.

In an act of final desperation his face contorted as he strained in an effort to force himself to rise slowly from his knees. With both legs from the knees down fully squashed and distended under his legs from the knees to the thighs, Rhodes began to rock back and forth like an orthodox Jew praying before the Wailing Wall in Jerusalem. His outstretched hands and outstretched fingers moved back and forth from his knees to the joints of his thighs in unified motion.

There he was. Albright Ambrose Rhodes. Chief Executive Officer. Owner. President.

Twenty Four

Suddenly both hands rose up from his knees and covered his eyes in grief. Ally and the senator lay in a heap of smoldering flesh just a few feet away from him. There was nothing he could do for them. Their fate was the same as his. But he could, at least try to save his loved ones who still had a chance.

He understood it now. It was absolutely certain that while you were still alive on the earth you had a spiritual choice to make for or against the Lord Jesus Christ. This choice could only be made while still alive. Albright had witnessed many heroic acts of valor on the beaches of Normandy and in France. Many had laid down their lives for others. Many had literally taken another man's bullet. This was his turn. He had to do something for them.

With renewed determination he stood to his feet and cupped both hands over his swollen mouth.

"Then, I beg of you, Sir! I plead with you, Father Abraham! I realize I no longer have any options left. My time has come. I have squandered the love of God. I have turned my back on the Lord Jesus Christ. I am guilty as charged. I stand before you a condemned man. "

His sobbing changed to a wail of despair.

"I beg of you. Please use your power and influence to send Billy Bob back down to earth. I know you can do it. I have read all about you. I admire you so much. You are my hero, Abraham. Everybody knows the battles you won. Please send Billy to visit with my brothers and my sister. There's also my sweet wife Ernestine. Not a bad bone in her body, Abraham. Look, just get her to sit down and listen to what our servant girl, Sue Ellen, had been trying to tell us all those years. Billy Bob too! Ask him. It's just that they were, well, so poor. I don't mean to be ugly. I really don't. But you must understand, Abraham. We were just in a different class. Our group was different. Please just send Billy, or anybody you think could do the job. It really doesn't matter to me. She'll listen if someone came back from the dead. It'll get her attention. And my family. None of them have given their hearts and lives to Jesus.

"And let me help you to understand why. You see, Father, the day and age we lived in was quite a bit different from your time. Don't misunderstand me. I'm not saying your generation didn't have all kinds of pressures and things. It must have been tough without cars and planes and all the modern conveniences. But life was simple for you folks. Church and religion was not only kind of mandated for you by your Rabbis and leaders, it gave you something to do. I mean you had no television or books to read and things like that. And you lived in a desert sort of place where there was not a whole lot of entertainment and activities except taking down tents and feeding the camels and goats and things like that."

Abraham held up his hand as if to speak. But Albright's adrenalin pounded at the seat of his emotions translating them into a most impassioned and desperate plea for mercy. He couldn't stop.

"Besides, Abraham, you guys had to toe the line. From the earliest age you did all kinds of rituals and you had to be able to recite the Torah from heart. And, hey, listen to this, all you had to do was offer sacrifices all the time. Abraham let me tell you something. You've got to help my family."

"They live in a lot of pressure. Time just flies by. Listen man, we had to keep up with other people. Our houses were not tents and things. We had cars and television. Just think about my kids. Abraham you wouldn't believe how much peer pressure there was on them. They had to wear the right clothes and go to the right schools. We, as parents, had to take care of them. I mean just think of the traffic jams. You should have seen it at five o'clock during rush hour. My business alone put me in board rooms and meetings all over the world, literally Abraham. One minute Washington, the next Minneapolis, the next Zurich, and the next Hong Kong. I mean it was exhausting. I'm telling you, Abraham. Just look at my family down there! They're all so busy. The kids are falling in love and dating and getting married. My brothers are all major business men with major responsibilities. Everyone wants a piece of them. My oldest niece and her new husband are trying to set up their home and establish themselves. And, you know how involved they all are in social ministry stuff. I mean they all give serious money and donations to charities, many of which are decidedly Christian and religious. My middle brother does even more than I did."

Abraham stopped him.

"I know, Albright. God, our Father receives so much pleasure and joy from countless numbers of His children who give in a wonderful way of the blessings He has given them. Much of His work in His church could not have been accomplished, humanly speaking, without precious men and women who were materially rich. That's exactly why God blessed them with money to begin with. And the more those people gave to God's work the more He gave to them. He knew He could trust them. I tell you, Albright, the whole time you were alive, the Lord Jesus was pleading for your soul. You came so close many times. But then you would back away. That's why the Lord Jesus said it would be harder for a rich man to enter the Kingdom of God thank for a camel to go through the eye of a needle!"

Makes sense now, thought the doomed man.

"You see, Albright, rich people see no need for God. They have everything, so to speak; both materially and humanly speaking. Why put trust in our Father? They operate only on the pleasure principle. What's in it for me? And so do others, even poor people. But we are dealing with you, now, Albright. That's why you have to recognize you are a sinner before a holy and righteous God, in order to be saved. And that salvation is made possible because of the obedience of the Son who went to a cruel Roman cross in order to make your reconciliation with our Father possible. This is why God was in Christ Jesus reconciling Himself to the world."

"We could go on but it is too late for you, Albright. God warned you. Once you die you face His judgment. You are in Hades for the time being but you will be sent to the lake of fire when you stand before the great white throne."

"When will that be?" Albright asked in a voice of quiet surrender mixed with soul-destroying horror at the very thought of what Abraham was saying to him.

"No one knows, but our Heavenly Father. Not even the Son."

"Surely even God would agree to send someone back from the dead? I mean have you even asked Him, Abraham? Genuinely? Look, if a man of your stature approached Him! Appeal to His grace and mercy. His sense of justice. Just think how that would put all those atheists and agnostics in their place! Doesn't God want everyone to be saved, anyway? I mean, Abraham, this would be the ultimate stroke of genius. Just imagine at church on Sunday morning. The preacher wouldn't have to say a thing. Just clap his hands and a whole bunch of dead people come walking out in front of the congregation. I mean everybody would believe in Jesus! Look I'd go. I mean it! I love my family so much I'd do anything. Even if I had to sign a contract agreeing that my eternal fate is sealed. I'd do it for them. Please, Abraham, just this one favor!"

Abraham seemed to look straight into his heart.

"You are quite correct about a lot of things you have said, Albright. God is who you said He is. He is just and merciful. He is love. He loves us so much He gave His only Son, the one who is totally unique, to become the sacrifice for our sin. That's why Jesus died on the cross. He gave His own life so that all men could have life. The devil, that old serpent who loves to call himself Lucifer Beelzebub, the first, of Babylon came to the world to rob, steal and destroy. He is the father of all lies. But Jesus came to give man life. A full and meaningful life. An abundant life. The Holy Spirit made this very clear to you, Albright. Besides, God gave you the Bible which is His Word. It is truth. Absolute truth. You are in hell, Albright, not because God sent you there, but because you chose to go there by refusing to accept the Lord Jesus Christ as your personal Lord and Savior!"

Rhodes just nodded his head.

"Now about your request to send someone back from the dead. I could not agree with you more. It would be hard to reject the reality of the love of God in the face of such a frightening confrontation. Unfortunately, and yet gloriously, it is not now, neither has it ever been, our choice to make. Our wonderful Heavenly Father makes all decisions regarding our well being. He alone is creator. He alone gives life, sustains life, takes life and guarantees the absolute certainty of life after death.

"So, actually, Albright, this is exactly what God decided to do. He brought the Lord Jesus back from the dead. Remember, Jesus had been in the grave for three days. Even Satan thought it was all over. But God raised Him from the dead on the third day. Even you made a habit of going to church on Easter Sunday. Churches all over the world are packed out on this Lord's Day. Why? Because even a man like yourself thought the occasion of Jesus' resurrection ought to be respected and honored. The difference was you never actually believed in your heart that God raised His Son from the dead. The resurrection of the Lord Jesus is what Christianity is all about. Every other religion known to man has some personality in the center. But not one of those religious figures has ever risen from the dead. They all died and were buried. Only the Son of God came back from the dead. He is alive for ever more.

"In short, Albright, because of the sin of Adam all people are dead in their trespasses and sins. There is no hope. Not for anyone. But because God raised Jesus from the dead all people who believe that and accept what God has done by faith, have life. Everlasting life. Like Billy Bob here, and myself. You never did believe in your heart, Albright. It was the proper thing for you to do to go to church from time to time. You played the part. Very well at times, I might add. But you could not pull the wool over God's eyes, so to speak. You never accepted Jesus as your personal Savior and Lord. You had to die to yourself. You had to give up on your own ability and surrender to the Lord Jesus Christ. He is a jealous God. He tolerates no rivalry or refusal or resignation, for that matter! He is an all or nothing

God. You are either on His team or you are not. There is no such thing as a "sort of" Christian, Albright.

"So God did give man someone who was raised back from the dead. It's been done. Jesus accomplished your very request, Albright. But you would not believe. So you have to pay the consequences. These are the wages of sin. If your name is not written the Lamb's Book of Life you will be cast into the lake of fire forever.

"Sending people like you and me back from the dead in addition to Jesus is not God's chosen method of evangelism. He now uses two primary methods to draw people into His heart. The first is the law of God as seen in and through His Word. You know His Word as the Bible. And just in case you want to compare our different generations again, Albright, let me put one on you. Your century enjoyed the whole revelation of Jesus Christ through the scriptures. You see, whereas in times past, like my time, God spoke through the prophets, to your generation He spoke through His Son. We often would get together and just marvel at the extent of God's grace to your people. Bibles everywhere. Every motel room, prisons, book stores, you name it. Especially in America. You even belonged to a Bible-believing church, Albright. Sunday by Sunday your pastor was faithful to expose and expound the truth of God's Word. You even studied about me when you were just a little fellow in Texas."

Albright thought about the numbers of Bibles he had in his house alone. When he died he still had the one given to him for his high school graduation. Just about every shelf seemed to have a Bible somewhere. Then there was the one in the guest living room he and Ernestine kept handy. They never read it for themselves. It was their emergency copy for unexpected visits by their pastor. Besides, in all honesty, Rhodes had no problem with the Bible. It was a good book to have around. He respected it and cared deeply about it. He never desecrated it or anything like that. It was a kind of "lucky charm" to have Bibles around, anyway. But when he did go to church, though, he would never carry one himself. It was sort of embarrassing for a man of his caliber to be seen with one in his hand. It was better for the women with their handbags and things. And when the pastor asked the congregation to open their Bibles to read the passage for the message, Albright preferred to sit and mind his own business. If the truth were known it kind of aggravated him, privately of course, when the preacher asked the people to get their Bibles out and, if they had not brought their own, to make use of the pew Bible. It just bothered Albright to be bothered. He was a busy man and Sunday mornings gave him a rare opportunity to not be bothered.

But now, as he listened to his death knell, things were so different. If only, he began to think in the midst of his pain. If only I had....but Abraham had more to say. "So, you see, Albright, the Bible was made available to you. Big time! You made a mockery of God's Word. And now you are paying for it.

"Not only does our Father give us the Word of God, but He gave us the Man of God. Beginning with the prophets and throughout the ages, God raised up His choice servants to be the couriers of His word. You had so many in your lifetime, Albright. None of them were perfect people. They were ordinary people. Sinners saved by the grace of God. The whole bunch of them, including me. Look how many times I let Jehovah down. But God chose some to be His mouthpiece. They are His chosen vessels. Your pastor was no exception, Albright. He was faithful to proclaim the Word of God. Some opposed him. Some left his church. Some made it very difficult for him. They silently and vocally persecuted him. They went after his family. But he did not relinquish his post. He stood firm. He preached with power and conviction. You were there. You heard him. Many times. But you were so wrapped up in your own world you never listened. You even said, albeit privately, that you considered all ministers to be people who could not do much else. It was kind of a last resort for them. And remember how you forbade your daughter from dating that young man who was studying for the ministry at the seminary in New Orleans? Any daughter of yours was going to marry well. Ministers and missionaries did not rise to your level of social acceptability, did they, Albright?

"But God sees it differently. This is His chosen method of evangelism. This is the means by which He tells the world about Himself. Then, the Holy Spirit, using the information provided by the Word of God though the man of God, draws all men into the heart of God. He convicts people of sin and of righteousness and of the coming judgment. This is God's decision, not ours!"

Albright sobbed and sobbed. He pleaded for his family, his friends, his brothers and sister.

"Please warn them. Otherwise they will also come into this place of torment!"

Abraham took Billy Bob by the shoulder and the two began to turn back towards the City of God. As they did so Abraham said, "I'm so sorry, Albright. If your loved ones do not listen to the man of God or the Word of God, there's not much any of us can do for them. If they do not pay attention to what they are hearing their opportunity to be saved might slip through their fingers. And it wouldn't make any difference even if someone in addition to Jesus were to rise from the dead. They would not be convinced."

Then they were gone.

Rhodes heard a voice. It was horrible. He spun around in the direction of Hades and the bottomless pit.

"So, you thought we wouldn't find you, did you?"

See You at the Finish Line

Like a Runner, we need Proper Training and Encouragement to make it to the Finish Line

Every Christian knows that life can be tough at the best of times! Just as the running of a race takes extreme effort–so it is that the Christian life is often a struggle–but one well worth the effort. The reality of life's journey can present major challenges!

Dr. Don Wilton uses the Book of Hebrews, while drawing on his personal journey, as a training manual for the race God has called us to run. As we maneuver the course and cross the finish line, we show others that living the Christian life really does make a difference. And that is what *See You at the Finish Line* is all about!

Despite the obstacles you encounter, keep your eyes on Jesus, the author and finisher of our faith. God has called you to run and He will be waiting for you at the finish line. He will welcome you with "well done, good and faithful servant."

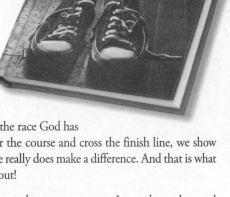